YOU'RE NOT ENTITLED TO YOUR OPINION
NO,

AF584949

EDITED BY
ALEXANDRA HANSEN

Thames & Hudson | THE CONVERSATION

We wish to acknowledge the Traditional Owners of the many lands on which these works were written, and the Wurundjeri people of the Kulin Nation on whose lands The Conversation's office is based. We pay our respects to all Aboriginal and Torres Strait Islander peoples and recognise they are the First Peoples of Australia.

First published in Australia in 2021
by Thames & Hudson Australia Pty Ltd
11 Central Boulevard, Portside Business Park
Port Melbourne, Victoria 3207
ABN: 72 004 751 964

thamesandhudson.com.au

These essays originally appeared on The Conversation (theconversation.com/au).

'Hidden women of history' (pp. 76–79): Kacey Sinclair acknowledges the research of Helen Harris OAM, whose book *The Right to Vote; the Right to Stand* (2014) presents a comprehensive history of women's involvement in local government in Victoria.

24 23 22 21 5 4 3 2

Thames & Hudson Australia wishes to acknowledge that Aboriginal and Torres Strait Islander people are the first storytellers of this nation and the traditional custodians of the land on which we live and work. We acknowledge their continuing culture and pay respect to Elders past, present and future.

978 1 760 76231 5 (paperback)
978 1 760 76238 4 (ebook)

A catalogue record for this book is available from the National Library of Australia

Cover design: Philip Campbell
Text design and typesetting: Patrick Cannon
Editing: Sarina Rowell
Printed and bound in Australia by McPherson's Printing Group

Contents

PART V A new philosophy

PART VI The decade in politics

PART VII Our natural world

Ten years of The Conversation

Misha Ketchell
Editor, The Conversation

During a recent radio interview, the host asked how editors know which articles on The Conversation will go viral. 'We don't,' I replied. 'We've got no idea, really. Anyone who says they do is kidding themselves.'

I felt like the Wizard of Oz after Toto pulled back the curtain. It used to be that editors were prized for having instinctive understanding of their readership. Their fat salaries (and similarly generous girths) owed everything to their ability to convince people that they possessed this magic ability.

Then along came the internet to show what people actually read and it taught us that editors have been kidding themselves. Many hard-hitting investigations and accounts of political scandals were sadly neglected by readers.

People were far more intellectually curious than we ever imagined, as well as being all-too predictably human: they clicked on stories about sex, celebrity, trivia, science, conspiracy theories, religion, philosophy and health, and human-interest stories.

Now the jig is up for editors who wish to thieve credit for the ideas they publish; you will find none of that here. If you admire anything in this collection of work from Australia's top academics, the credit belongs to the authors, who have dedicated their working lives to the pursuit of knowledge conveyed so crisply in these pages.

Having said that, this book is a celebration of the best work from the first ten years of The Conversation, and I do want to take this opportunity to tell you a little about how this unique publisher came into being.

The Conversation launched in Melbourne in 2011, with a mission to work with academics to bring about better-informed public discourse. Our method is to use our journalism skills to help experts share their knowledge directly with the public. It is based on win–win outcomes that flow from real collaboration.

We never imagined – in those early days of crowding around a desk, trying to convince academics to write articles at short notice – that we'd end up where we are today. The Conversation is now a global network of editorial teams that employs more than 100 journalists.

Academics value The Conversation because we help them make a difference. They love being able to offer solutions to complex problems, and to be heard by politicians, public servants and members of the public.

Journalists value The Conversation because it provides a quick way to find people who know what they're talking about. Editors like that our work is free to republish, and our authors can add context and depth to news coverage. Radio and TV producers use The Conversation to find interviewees who have something to offer.

Readers value it too. The Conversation was conceived as an antidote to shrinking newsrooms and a changing media landscape that gives oxygen to misinformation and seeks out the shrill over the sober. It is useful for anyone who wants trustworthy information: from students looking to quote professors, to policy makers who want to bone up on the latest research.

Under the bonnet, our work is powered by new technology and old-school values: respect, curiosity, courtesy. We rely on the help of all the generous and public-spirited people who share our values.

I want to thank the Australian university leaders who had the foresight to back an idea, especially those who have been with us since we launched: take a bow, the University of Melbourne, Monash University, the University of Technology Sydney, the University of Western Australia and the Australian National University. Thanks also to the CSIRO and the Victorian and federal governments, for having the vision and guts to contribute seed funding; and to the Commonwealth Bank, for its generous early support of our technology platform.

Thanks to the many foundations and funders who have understood the value of reliable information in solving big problems. Thanks to Jack Rejtman and Andrew Jaspan, who together co-founded The Conversation. Thanks to our colleagues in journalism, here and overseas, and to all the selfless academics who drop everything in their already busy lives to write for us.

Finally, thanks to Alexandra Hansen, our peerless Chief of Staff, who has worked tirelessly to curate this collection. Being asked to select the top articles is rather like being asked to choose favourites among one's children – you love them all, differently.

Somehow, Alexandra has managed to navigate the tug of these competing loyalties to come up with this elegant collection. I hope you get as much knowledge and pleasure from reading it as we did from curating it.

A decade of disruption and disaster

Michelle Grattan
Professorial Fellow, University of Canberra

The world was transformed in the decade between 2011 and 2021, The Conversation's first ten years.

In the change that may carry the most far-reaching implications for the future, these years saw a massive shift internationally, with an assertive and increasingly aggressive China flexing its economic, political and military muscle.

Xi Jinping became China's all-powerful leader in 2012. In 2021 the United States and other countries were struggling to deal with the consequences of his nationalistic reset.

For Australia, China's ascendancy carried major implications for our region, our security and our trade, which have a long way to play out.

Within the decade, Australia–China relations went from cooperative and promising to openly antagonistic – from Prime Minister Julia Gillard announcing a strategic partnership in 2013, to China refusing to return Australian ministers' calls just a few years later.

In 2021, the Australian government cancelled Victorian agreements under China's Belt and Road Initiative, and China suspended activity under the China–Australia Strategic Economic Dialogue.

Coincidentally, it was from China that came the start of the world pandemic, a modern plague unlike anything seen for a century, which wrapped the end of the decade in catastrophe.

COVID-19 stress-tested nations, and many were overwhelmed, as millions died worldwide and countries plunged into recession.

Thanks to the luck of its island geography, which facilitated a closed international border, and strong decision-making in both health and economic policy, Australia (as of mid-2021) proved up to the pandemic's challenges.

This was despite Victoria's second wave, which cost hundreds of lives among nursing home residents, and the glitches and delays with the national vaccine rollout.

Coping with the pandemic realigned – in practical rather than formal constitutional terms – Australia's federation, with premiers and chief ministers often acting independently, especially in closing their borders.

This devolution of power happened at the same time as Prime Minister Scott Morrison's creation of a national cabinet achieved a united approach on many fronts.

At the start of the decade, the world was still coping with the aftermath of the Global Financial Crisis. The 'Great Recession', as it was dubbed, had wrought havoc, and shaken and reshaped financial institutions.

But Australia, thanks to its mining exports to China, and the Rudd Labor government's spending blitz, had managed to sandbag itself against falling into recession.

The financial crisis had elevated the role of government. It had also seen the emergence of the G20 as a leaders' forum, for which Kevin Rudd pushed, giving Australia a stronger voice internationally.

In Western democracies, the GFC intensified people's loss of trust in political leaders and institutions, a longer-term trend (reversed, at least for the moment, in Australia in the pandemic). In many countries, it dealt a blow to faith in market forces and globalisation.

The period 2011–21 was not a happy one for democracy and societal cohesion in the West. As technologies changed work and national economies, swathes of people felt left behind and marginalised. Communities, and nations, became inward-looking. Populism flourished in this fertile environment.

In Britain, resentment against what were seen as the impositions of the European Union resulted in the unexpected success of the Brexit vote.

In the US, Donald Trump cast himself as the political outsider, and triumphed, also unexpectedly, over Hillary Clinton, the ultimate political insider, who had been favoured to become America's first female president at the 2016 election.

In his four years in the White House, Trump delivered chaos that rippled through the wider world. The American political system, already dysfunctional, was strained almost to breaking point. Perceptions of American omnipotence and international engagement, already eroding, were undermined further by Trump's 'America First' stance.

Unpredictability, incompetence and vendettas distorted presidential decision-making, seen at its worst during the pandemic.

In Australia, politics did become more populist, but it avoided the extremes and splits of the US, thanks to better economic circumstances, less inequality, and a more politically homogeneous polity (in part due to compulsory voting).

Prime ministers Malcolm Turnbull and Morrison dealt with Trump as best they could. Turnbull pitched to him as a fellow businessman and, in a difficult phone call, persuaded him to honour an earlier deal for the US to take hundreds of Australia's offshore refugees.

Morrison – unusually among world leaders – was a Trump favourite, honoured with a state dinner. He went with the flow.

Between 2011 and 2021, the US turned full circle. In 2011 Barack Obama, America's first Black president, was readying for a second term, although the glow of optimism around him had faded and the US was headed for the disillusionment that culminated in Trump's election.

At the end of the ten years, after the Trump tornado had blown itself out, some normality was restored. Despite Morrison's good relationship with Trump, in Canberra there was a sigh of relief when Joe Biden was elected.

Biden, seventy-eight when inaugurated, had no time to waste. Favoured with a Senate majority, he pushed through a massive stimulus package for the pandemic-ravaged US economy.

In Australia, the Coalition government had taken the budget deeply into the red in 2020, with its generous JobKeeper wage subsidy scheme, higher welfare payments and financial backing for businesses (though universities, badly hit by plummeting foreign student numbers, were left relatively in the cold).

The 2021 budget also eschewed the Coalition's previous abhorrence of 'debt and deficit'. Liberal icon John Howard had told the government early on, 'in times of crisis there are no ideological constraints'.

Despite dire predictions that unemployment could rise to the mid teens, Australia's pandemic trajectory was V-shaped. The bounce-back was strong and unemployment was contained, fuelling an ambition to drive the jobless rate well below 5 per cent, in an effort to push up stagnant wages.

One of the first articles published by The Conversation was from economist Ross Garnaut and titled, 'When the science is so clear, why is the argument so clouded?'

Climate change was a constant issue through the decade. Naysayers notwithstanding, the science was widely accepted. Reaching solutions was another matter.

Progress was frustratingly sporadic, with steps forward, steps back. Hopes had been dashed in 2009 at Copenhagen. In 2015 they were revived in Paris. Then Trump took the US out of the Paris Agreement. By 2021, optimism returned. Biden had America back in the game and was driving the agenda hard in the run-up to the November 2021 Glasgow Conference.

For Australia, the debate over climate and energy has been a first-order political disruptor. It helped weaken Gillard's prime ministership, and Tony Abbott scrapped Labor's carbon price scheme. Turnbull was committed to progress but could not overcome the resistance within the Coalition; eventually, his efforts contributed centrally to his downfall. The Labor opposition was on the back foot on these issues at the 2019 election.

Biden's presidency put pressure on Australia to be more ambitious; as of mid-2021 Morrison was creeping towards embracing a target of net zero emissions by 2050.

The decade 2011–21, during which identity politics became more all-pervasive, saw significant social movements coming out of the US.

#MeToo mobilised women internationally, and had its reverberations in Australia, with allegations of misbehaviour levelled against some high-profile men.

Black Lives Matter demonstrations found their echo around the world and locally, feeding into renewed pressure over deaths in custody and the high rate of Indigenous incarceration.

But progress on Indigenous issues was slow. Abbott was anxious for a referendum for constitutional recognition, but this proposal, although supported by both sides of politics, has been bogged down in the detail and overwhelmed by more ambitious Indigenous agendas.

The alleged rape of a Coalition staffer, Brittany Higgins, by a colleague in Parliament House, and an allegation of historical rape against senior Coalition minister Christian Porter led to a flurry of government initiatives in 2021 directed to women. Whether outcomes will match undertakings remains to be seen.

For much of the decade, attempts to legalise marriage equality in Australia ran into a brick wall. Finally, in 2017 the law was changed, after a postal ballot showed strong support. Community opinion had been ahead of the caution of politicians on both sides.

For Australia, 2011–21 was a decade of mixed economic results, reform fatigue and, at least until the pandemic, mostly indifferent political leadership.

Largely because it is so blessed with resources (and thanks to large-scale immigration), Australia enjoyed nearly three decades without a recession, until COVID hit.

But the nation's leaders could not recapture the reform drive of the Hawke–Keating years of the 1980s and early 1990s, or even the more limited effort of Prime Minister John Howard, who introduced the GST.

To a considerable extent Australia squandered the enormous returns of the mining boom: for example, in failing to create a sovereign wealth fund (other than for the limited purpose of paying pensions to retired public servants).

Australia's economic performance, particularly in the second half of the decade, was ordinary. Economist Saul Eslake has calculated that between the end of the early 1990s recession and the GFC's onset, productivity growth accounted for over half (54 per cent) of Australia's economic growth, while increases in 'labour supply' (more people in the labour force, lower unemployment and more average hours worked) accounted for the rest. But from the end of the mining boom (2015) to the start of the pandemic, productivity growth accounted for just 28 per cent of Australia's (much lower) growth.

The failure of leadership was on both sides of politics; prime ministers came and went on the whim of factions and the prevailing (but often temporary) wisdom of opinion polls.

Julia Gillard had deposed Rudd in 2010. As Australia's first female PM, Gillard's arrival at the top seemed to hold historic promise. But the way she grabbed power, and Rudd's determination to seize it back, dogged her prime ministership. Her legacy includes the National Disability Insurance Scheme but the hopes held for her were not fulfilled.

Abbott's skills lay in negative campaigning rather than positive governing, and he could not retain the support of his party against the undermining by Turnbull, whom Abbott had displaced in opposition.

A charismatic character, Turnbull seemed in tune with where modern Australia should be. But for the second time, his leadership collapsed under a combination of personal flaws and internal splits over energy and climate policy.

Morrison came through the middle of the face-off between Turnbull and right-wing aspirant Peter Dutton.

Despite his manifest ambition, Morrison was the accidental federal leader of the decade. But circumstances favoured him.

He won the 'unwinnable' 2019 election through a combination of canny campaigning and an opposition carrying over-heavy policy baggage, with an unpopular leader.

Then the politics of the pandemic worked for incumbents who performed well.

No election is guaranteed, and circumstances can change quickly. But by mid 2021, Morrison appeared to have set himself up for the next election, while coming across as a political manager rather than a man with a vision for the nation.

When The Conversation began, its rationale was to tap into Australia's universities to bring to readers fact-based informed analysis, written by experts.

It launched in a media landscape in which the old players were being challenged by the immense disruption of the new digital world.

As advertising migrated online and websites proliferated, the business model of the legacy media was shattered.

The new media meant more choice. The total amount of media content expanded exponentially. But quality and responsibility were compromised, and the power of tech giants became an urgent issue.

Social media was hyped as giving everyone who wanted it a say. The reality was this 'say' often debased the social and political conversation. Social media put the angry on steroids.

Over the decade, media have become even more central to politics. But how the political class uses media has changed to exploit new opportunities. These days, politicians can appeal directly to their audiences via social media. This, combined with contemporary sophisticated databases and research tools, allows for highly targeted – often extremely reactive – campaigning.

In this new world, paradoxically, 'facts' can be harder to establish and agree on, despite everyone having many more ways of chasing them down.

But, certainly, 'experts' have come into their own here in Australia during the pandemic, in guiding both the health response and the economic lifeline. Suddenly the decision-makers realised the shocking truth – how unmoored they were in this alarming situation – and they relied on the specialists for advice. Meanwhile, the public looked to people they believed they could trust. It was not all plain sailing for the experts, however, who argued among themselves and also found they were dragged into the political debates.

Editor's note

Alexandra Hansen

On selecting which essays would make up this 'best of the best', I contacted current, and some former, editors from all nine editions of The Conversation (Africa, Australia, Canada, Spain, France, Indonesia, New Zealand, the United Kingdom and United States) and asked them to send me the pieces they are most proud of from their time at The Conversation: the pieces that really put their edition on the map, and that made a big impact.

I also looked at our most-read pieces, some of which have had 8 or 9 million unique page views.

From this list of about 200, I whittled down the contents to the fifty absolute best examples of what we do – while trying to include a range of subjects, big news events, and pieces from every edition. Reading through ten years of groundbreaking, heartwarming, and sometimes heartbreaking, work made me fall in love all over again with what I do. I hope you enjoy reading them as much as I enjoyed choosing them.

PART I

Challenging the orthodoxy

Slavery in America: Back in the headlines

Daina Ramey Berry
Oliver H Radkey Regents Professor of History, University of Texas at Austin

21 October 2014

People think they know everything about slavery in the United States, but they don't. They think the majority of African slaves came to the American colonies, but they didn't. They talk about 400 years of slavery, but it wasn't. They claim all southerners owned slaves, but they didn't. Some argue it was a long time ago, but it wasn't.

Slavery has been in the news a lot lately. Perhaps it's because of the increase in human trafficking on American soil or the headlines about income inequality, the mass incarceration of African-Americans or discussions about reparations to the descendants of slaves. Several publications have fuelled these conversations: Ta-Nehisi Coates's 'The Case for Reparations' in *The Atlantic Monthly*, French economist Thomas Piketty's *Capital in the Twenty-First Century*, historian Edward Baptist's *The Half Has Never Been Told: Slavery and The Making of American Capitalism*, and law professor Bryan A Stevenson's *Just Mercy: A Story of Justice and Redemption*.

As a scholar of slavery at the University of Texas at Austin, I welcome the public debates and connections the American people are making with history. However, there are still many misconceptions about slavery.

I've spent my career dispelling myths about 'the peculiar institution'. The goal in my courses is not to victimise one group and celebrate another. Instead, we trace the history of slavery in all its forms to make sense of the origins of wealth inequality and the roots of discrimination today. The history of slavery provides deep context to contemporary conversations and counters the distorted facts, internet hoaxes and poor scholarship I caution my students against.

Four myths about slavery

Myth one: The majority of African captives came to what became the United States

Truth: only 380,000 or 4–6 per cent came to the United States. The majority of enslaved Africans went to Brazil, followed by the Caribbean.

A significant number of enslaved Africans arrived in the American colonies by way of the Caribbean, where they were 'seasoned' and mentored into slave life. They spent months or years recovering from the harsh realities of the Middle Passage. Once they were forcibly accustomed to slave labour, many were then brought to plantations on American soil.

Myth two: Slavery lasted for 400 years

Popular culture is rich with references to 400 years of oppression. There seems to be confusion between the Transatlantic Slave Trade (1440–1888) and the institution of slavery, confusion only reinforced by the Bible, Genesis 15:13: 'Then the Lord said to him, "Know for certain that for four hundred years your descendants will be strangers in a country not their own and that they will be enslaved and mistreated there."'

Listen to Lupe Fiasco – just one hip-hop artist to refer to the 400 years – in his 2011 imagining of America without slavery, 'All Black Everything'.

Truth: slavery was not unique to the United States; it is a part of almost every nation's history, from Greek and Roman civilisations to contemporary forms of human trafficking. The American part of the story lasted fewer than 400 years.

How do we calculate it? Most historians use 1619 as a starting point: twenty Africans referred to as 'servants' arrived in Jamestown, Virginia, on a Dutch ship. It's important to note, however, that they were not the first Africans on American soil. Africans first arrived in America in the late 16th century, not as slaves but as explorers, together with Spanish and Portuguese explorers. One of the best known of these African 'conquistadors' was Estevanico, who travelled throughout the south-east, from present-day Florida to Texas. As far as the institution of chattel slavery – the treatment of slaves as property – in the United States goes, if we use 1619 as the beginning and the 1865 Thirteenth Amendment as the end, then it lasted 246 years, not 400.

Myth three: All southerners owned slaves

Truth: roughly 25 per cent of all southerners owned slaves. The fact that one quarter of the southern population were slaveholders is still shocking to many. This truth brings historical insight to modern conversations about the Occupy movement, its challenge to the inequality gap and its slogan 'we are the 99%'.

Take the case of Texas. When it established statehood, the Lone Star State had a shorter period of Anglo-American chattel slavery than other southern states – only 1845 to 1865 – because Spain and Mexico had occupied the region for almost one half of the 19th century with policies that either abolished or limited slavery. Still, the number of people impacted by wealth and income inequality is staggering. By 1860, the Texas enslaved population was 182,566, but slaveholders represented 27 per cent of the population, controlled 68 per cent of the government positions and 73 per cent of the wealth. Shocking figures, but today's income gap in Texas is arguably more stark, with 10 per cent of tax filers taking home 50 per cent of the income.

Myth four: Slavery was a long time ago
Truth: African-Americans have been free in this country for less time than they were enslaved. Do the maths: Blacks have been free for 149 years, which means that most Americans are two to three generations removed from slavery. However, former slaveholding families have built their legacies on the institution and generated wealth that African-Americans have not been privy to because enslaved labour was forced; segregation maintained wealth disparities; and overt and covert discrimination limited African-American recovery efforts.

The value of slaves

Economists and historians have examined detailed aspects of the enslaved experience for as long as slavery existed. Recent publications related to slavery and capitalism explore economic aspects of cotton production and offer commentary on the amount of wealth generated from enslaved labour.

My own work enters this conversation looking at the value of individual slaves and the ways enslaved people responded to being treated as a commodity. They were bought and sold just like we sell cars and cattle today. They were gifted, deeded and mortgaged the same way we sell houses today. They were itemised and insured the same way we manage our assets and protect our valuables.

Enslaved people were subject to valuation at every stage of their lives, from before birth until after death. Slaveholders examined women for their fertility and projected the value of their 'future increase'. As slaves grew up, enslavers assessed their value through a rating system that quantified their work. An 'A1 Prime hand' was one term used for a 'first-rate' slave who could do the most work in a given day. Their value decreased on a quarter scale, from three-fourths hands to one-fourth hands, to a rate of zero, which was typically reserved for elderly or differently abled bondpeople (another term for slaves).

Guy and Andrew, two prime males sold in 1859 at the largest auction in US history, commanded different prices. Although similar in 'all marketable points in size, age, and skill', Guy commanded $1280 while Andrew sold for $1040 because 'he had lost his right eye'. A reporter from the *New York Tribune* noted 'that the market value of the right eye in the Southern country is $240'. Enslaved bodies were reduced to monetary values assessed from year to year, and sometimes from month to month, for their entire lifespan and beyond. By today's standards, Andrew and Guy would be worth about $33,000–$40,000.

Slavery was an extremely diverse economic institution; one that extracted unpaid labour out of people in a variety of settings, from small single-crop farms and plantations to urban universities. This diversity is also reflected in their prices.

Enslaved people understood they were treated as commodities. 'I was sold away from mammy at three years old,' recalled Harriett Hill of Georgia. 'I remembers it! It lack selling a calf from the cow,' she shared in a 1930s interview with the Works Progress Administration. 'We are human beings,' she told her interviewer. Those in bondage understood their status. Even though Harriet Hill was too little to remember her price when she was three, she recalled being sold for $1400 at age nine or ten: 'I never could forget it.'

Slavery in popular culture

Slavery is part and parcel of American popular culture but for more than thirty years the television mini-series *Roots* was the primary visual representation of the institution, except for a handful of independent (and not widely known) films such as Haile Gerima's *Sankofa* or the Brazilian movie *Quilombo*. Today, Steve McQueen's *12 Years a Slave* is a box office success, actress Azie Mira Dungey has a popular web series called *Ask a Slave*, and in *Cash Crop!* sculptor Stephen Hayes compares the slave ships of the 18th century with third world sweatshops.

From the serious – PBS's award-winning *The African Americans: Many Rivers to Cross*; and the interactive Slave Dwelling Project, whereby school-aged children spend the night in slave cabins – to the comic, on *Saturday Night Live*, slavery is today front and centre.

The elephant that sits at the centre of our history is coming into focus. American slavery happened – we are still living with its consequences.

Jesus wasn't white. He was a brown-skinned, Middle Eastern Jew. Here's why that matters

Robyn J Whitaker
Bromby Senior Lecturer in Biblical Studies, Trinity College, University of Divinity

29 March 2018

I grew up in a Christian home, where a photo of Jesus hung on my bedroom wall. I still have it. It is schmaltzy and rather tacky in that 1970s kind of way, but as a little girl I loved it. In this picture, Jesus looks kind and gentle; he gazes down at me lovingly. He is also light-haired, blue-eyed and very white.

The problem is, Jesus was not white. You'd be forgiven for thinking otherwise if you've ever entered a Western church or visited an art gallery. But while there is no physical description of him in the Bible, there is also no doubt that the historical Jesus, the man who was executed by the Roman state in the 1st century CE, was a brown-skinned, Middle Eastern Jew.

This is not controversial from a scholarly point of view, but somehow it is a forgotten detail for many of the millions of Christians who will gather to celebrate Easter this week.

On Good Friday, Christians attend churches to worship Jesus and, in particular, remember his death on a cross. In most of these churches, Jesus will be depicted as a white man, a guy who looks like Anglo-Australians, a guy who's easy for other Anglo-Australians to identify with.

Think for a moment of the rather dashing Jim Caviezel, who played Jesus in Mel Gibson's *The Passion of the Christ*. He is an Irish-American actor. Or call to mind some of the most famous artworks of Jesus's crucifixion – Ruben, Grunewald, Giotto – and again we see the European bias in depicting a white-skinned Jesus.

Does any of this matter? Yes, it really does. As a society, we are well aware of the power of representation and the importance of diverse role models.

After winning the 2013 Oscar for Best Supporting Actress for her role in *12 Years a Slave*, Kenyan actress Lupita Nyong'o shot to fame. In interviews since then, Nyong'o has repeatedly articulated her feelings of inferiority as a young woman because all the images of beauty she saw around her were of lighter-skinned women. It was only when she saw the fashion world embracing Sudanese model Alek Wek that she realised black could be beautiful too.

If we can recognise the importance of ethnically and physically diverse role models in our media, why can't we do the same with faith? Why do we continue to allow images of a whitened Jesus to dominate?

Many churches and cultures do depict Jesus as a brown or Black man. Orthodox Christians usually have a very different iconography from that of European art – if you enter a church in Africa, you'll likely see an African Jesus on display.

But these are rarely the images we see in Australian Protestant and Catholic churches, and it is our loss. It allows the mainstream Christian community to separate their devotion to Jesus from compassionate regard for those who look different.

I would even go so far as to say it creates a cognitive disconnect, where one can feel deep affection for Jesus but little empathy for a Middle Eastern person. It likewise has implications for the theological claim that humans are made in God's image. If God is always imagined as white, then the default human becomes white, and such thinking undergirds racism.

Historically, the whitewashing of Jesus contributed to Christians being some of the worst perpetrators of anti-Semitism and it continues to manifest in the 'othering' of non-Anglo-Saxon Australians.

This Easter, I can't help but wonder, what would our church and society look like if we just remembered that Jesus was brown? If we were confronted with the reality that the body hung on the cross was a brown body: one broken, tortured and publicly executed by an oppressive regime.

How might it change our attitudes if we could see that the unjust imprisonment, abuse and execution of the historical Jesus has more in common with the experience of Indigenous Australians or asylum seekers than it does with those who hold power in the church and usually represent Christ?

Perhaps most radical of all, I can't help but wonder what might change if we were more mindful that the person Christians celebrate as God in the flesh and saviour of the entire world was not a white man, but a Middle Eastern Jew.

FactCheck: Are children 'better off' with a mother and father than with same-sex parents?

Jennifer Power
Senior Research Fellow at the Australian Research Centre in Sex, Health and Society, La Trobe University

Reviewed by Simon Crouch
Honorary Researcher, Jack Brockhoff Child Health and Wellbeing Program, University of Melbourne

7 September 2017

Public campaigns for and against same-sex marriage have been heightened by the Turnbull government's plan to conduct a $122 million voluntary postal survey asking the nation whether same-sex couples should be able to marry under Australian law. Discussing his opposition to same-sex marriage, Liberal MP Kevin Andrews said on Sky News, 13 August 2017, 'Optimally, you've got the input from both [a mother and a father] and the children brought up in those circumstances are, as a cohort, better off than those who are not ... whether it's in terms of health outcomes, mental health, physical health, whether it's in terms of employment prospects, in terms of how this is generated from one generation to another, the social science evidence is overwhelmingly in one direction in this regard.'

Let's look at the research.

Checking the source

When asked for sources to support his statements, a spokesperson for Kevin Andrews told The Conversation: 'Mr Andrews wrote a book called

Maybe I Do. You might also like to look at the 2011 report, *For Kids' Sake*, by Professor Patrick Parkinson of the University of Sydney and studies by Douglas Allen (2015) in Canada and Paul Sullins (2015) in the US.'

Verdict

Kevin Andrews's assertion that children who are brought up with a mother and father are 'as a cohort, better off than those who are not' is not supported by research evidence.

The majority of research on this topic shows that children or adolescents raised by same-sex parents fare equally as well as those raised by opposite-sex parents on a wide range of social, emotional, health and academic outcomes.

Response to Kevin Andrews's sources

First of all, let's look at the sources provided by Kevin Andrews's spokesperson to support his statements. A summary of Andrews's book on the National Library of Australia website says it: '... reviews the evidence on the benefits of marriage for society, children, and adults. It argues that healthy, stable, and happy marriages are the optimal institution for promoting individual well-being and healthy societies.'

It's true there is a large body of evidence to show stability in marriage and family life is beneficial for children, particularly in early childhood. Some research has shown these benefits are associated with higher average income and education levels among married couples, rather than marriage itself.

But these studies didn't involve comparisons between opposite-sex and same-sex married couples, so they do not defend the argument that heterosexual marriage leads to better outcomes for children than same-sex marriage. In fact, some research suggests same-sex marriage would provide benefits for children being raised in these families.

Patrick Parkinson's report, *For Kids' Sake*, links rising rates of divorce, family conflict and instability in parental relationships with increasing psychological distress among young people in Australia. One of Parkinson's conclusions was that: 'the most stable, safe and nurturing environment for children is when their parents are, and remain, married to one another'.

There are studies that support these assertions. This research supports the importance of family stability, quality relationships between parents and children, and the need for access to socioeconomic resources – but not the need for parents to be heterosexual.

Douglas Allen's 2015 paper, 'More heat than light: A critical assessment of the same-sex parenting literature, 1995–2013', is a critical, but not systematic, review of more than sixty studies relating to same-sex parenting and/or child outcomes. This paper does not present findings related to child outcomes.

Rather, Allen says that, due to sampling bias and small sample sizes in the existing body of work, there is currently no conclusive scientific evidence demonstrating children raised by same-sex couples do better or worse than children raised by heterosexual couples.

Andrews's spokesperson also pointed to 2015 research from Paul Sullins. Sullins's 2015 analysis of data from the US National Health Interview Survey indicated children raised by same-sex parents were more than twice as likely to experience emotional problems than those raised by heterosexual, married parents who were biologically related to their children. But this analysis was criticised for not taking into account the stability of the family environment.

The author combined all children in same-sex families into one category, while placing children in opposite-sex families into separate categories – including different categories for step-parents and single parents, for example. So, the comparison made was between *all* same-sex parented families and a *selection* of *stable* heterosexual families.

Research on outcomes for children in same-sex parented families

Now let's look at other studies that have been conducted around the world. Many of these studies examine the outcomes for children in same-sex parented families where both parents are women. There has been comparatively little research on families in which both parents are men. It can be difficult to achieve adequate sample sizes of children raised in two-father families, given the small number of these families. There is no research showing that children raised by gay fathers fare worse than other children.

A study published in 2016 using data from the US National Survey of Children's Health for 2011–12 compared outcomes for children aged six to seventeen years in ninety-five female same-sex parented families and ninety-five opposite-sex parented families. (See 'Same-sex and different-sex parent households and child health outcomes' by Henny M Bos et al.)

The study found no differences in outcomes for children raised by lesbian parents compared with heterosexual parents on a range of outcomes, including general health, emotional difficulties, coping behaviour and learning behaviour.

A paper published for the American Sociological Association in 2014 reviewed ten years of scientific literature on child wellbeing in same-sex parented families in the US. The literature review covered forty original published studies, including numerous credible and methodologically sound social science studies, many of which drew on nationally representative data.

The authors concluded there was clear consensus in scientific literature that children raised by same-sex couples fared as well as children raised by opposite-sex couples. This applied to a range of wellbeing measures, including:

- academic performance
- cognitive development
- social development
- psychological health
- early sexual activity
- substance abuse.

The authors noted differences in child wellbeing were largely due to socioeconomic circumstances and family stability.

A meta-analysis published in the *Journal of Marriage and Family* in 2010 combined the results of thirty-three studies to assess how the gender of parents affected children. (See 'How does the gender of parents matter?' by Timothy J Biblarz and Judith Stacey.) The authors found the strengths typically associated with married mother-father families appeared to the same degree in families with two mothers and potentially in those with two fathers.

The meta-analysis found no evidence children raised by same-sex couples fared worse than children raised by opposite-sex couples on a range of outcomes, including:

- security of attachment to parents

- behavioural problems
- self-perceptions of cognitive and physical competence
- interest, effort and success in school.

This review included studies from Europe, the UK and the US. The authors said scholars had achieved: 'a rare degree of consensus that unmarried lesbian parents are raising children who develop at least as well as their counterparts with married heterosexual parents.'

In Australia, a large study published in the peer-reviewed *BMC Public Health* journal in 2014 (and of which I was one of five co-authors) surveyed 315 parents representing 500 children. (See 'Parent-reported measures of child health and wellbeing in same-sex parent families: A cross-sectional survey' by Simon R Crouch et al.) Eighty per cent of children had a female same-sex attracted parent, while 18 per cent had a male same-sex attracted parent.

The results did support previous research showing that stigma related to a parent's sexual orientation is negatively associated with mental health and wellbeing.

But, overall, the study found children and adolescents raised by same-sex parents in Australia fared as well as children of opposite-sex parents, and better on measures of general behaviour, general health and family cohesion.

A follow-up paper published in 2016 ('Impact of family structure and socio-demographic characteristics on child health and wellbeing in same-sex parent families: A cross-sectional survey' by Simon Robert Crouch et al.) found there was no difference between children raised in female same-sex parent households and children raised in male same-sex parent households.

Further work from the same project reported on surveys and interviews with adolescents raised by same-sex parents. This study (of which I was one of four co-authors) did find some adolescents with same-sex parents reported experiencing anxiety relating to fear of discrimination, which was linked to poorer wellbeing. (See 'The health perspectives of Australian adolescents from same-sex parent families: A mixed methods study' by SR Crouch et al.)

A US study published in 2011 ('Substance use by adolescents of the USA National Longitudinal Lesbian Family Study' by Naomi G Goldberg et al.) found adolescents raised by lesbian mothers were more likely to have reported occasional substance use, but not more likely to have reported heavy use, than other adolescents.

A 2010 analysis of data from the 2000 US census found children raised by same-sex couples had no fundamental deficits in making normal progress through school compared with children raised by opposite-sex couples. (See 'Nontraditional families and childhood progress through school' by Michael J Rosenfeld.)

When parents' socioeconomic status and the characteristics of the students were accounted for, the educational outcomes for children of same-sex couples couldn't be distinguished with statistical certainty from those for children of heterosexual married couples.

Analysing studies that show different results

Some studies have indicated adults raised by same-sex parents fare worse on some educational, social or emotional outcomes. But the *majority* of research does not support this. There are also studies that have been published and later discredited but continue to be used as references.

The 2012 US New Family Structures Study, also known as the 'Regnerus study', is often cited by groups opposed to same-sex marriage.

The study looked at outcomes for adults aged eighteen to thirty-nine. It compared outcomes for adults with a parent who had had a same-sex relationship with outcomes for adults raised by still-married, heterosexual couples who were biologically related to their children. It showed the adults with a gay or lesbian parent or parents fared worse on a range of social, educational and health outcomes. But this study has been very widely criticised.

In a brief filed in the US Supreme Court in 2015, the American Sociological Association said: 'The Regnerus study ... did not specifically examine children raised by same-sex parents, and provides no support for the conclusions that same-sex parents are inferior parents or that the children of same-sex parents experience worse outcomes.'

As outlined by the American Sociological Association, the study removed all divorced, single and step-parent families from the heterosexual group, leaving only stable, married, heterosexual families as the comparison. In addition, Regnerus categorised children as having been raised by a parent in a same-sex relationship 'regardless of whether they were in fact raised by the parent ... and regardless of the amount of time that they spent under the parent's care.'

A subsequent reanalysis of the data, using different criteria for categorising respondents, found the results inconclusive, or suggestive that 'adult children raised by same-sex two-parent families show a comparable adult profile to their peers raised by two-biological-parent families'. (See 'A "reality check" for the Regnerus study on gay parenting' by Dale Carpenter.)

Strengths and weaknesses of evidence on outcomes for children

The 'gold standard' for research on child and family outcomes are studies that involve randomly selected, population-based samples. This has been difficult to achieve in research on same-sex parenting because many population-based studies don't ask about parents' sexual orientation. Even where they do ask, not all studies include a sample of children or adults raised by same-sex parents that is large enough to provide for reliable statistical analysis.

This has led to criticism of the quality of evidence on outcomes for children raised by same-sex parents, because most studies have relied on convenience or volunteer samples, which are not randomly selected, and so may include bias.

However, there are methodological limitations in all studies. And, as outlined earlier, recent analyses of population-based data sets have supported the finding that children or adolescents raised by same-sex couples do not experience poorer outcomes than other children. So there is no clear basis to the argument that convenience samples lead to 'incorrect' findings due to bias.

Review

This FactCheck gives a good broad overview of the research and scientific consensus in regard to child health and wellbeing in same-sex parent families. The studies included, on balance, represent the current understanding of academics and child health experts on child health and wellbeing outcomes in same-sex parent families.

The National Lesbian Longitudinal Family Study provides additional evidence to support the verdict of this FactCheck. As a well-established and methodologically robust longitudinal study, the National Lesbian Longitudinal Family Study provides important additional insights.

In the Australian context, the 2013 Australian Institute of Family Studies review of same-sex parent families also supports the overall verdict of this FactCheck.

It should be noted that research has indicated same-sex parent families experience stigma and discrimination, and when they do, it can impact on child health and wellbeing.

Overall, however, the verdict in this FactCheck is appropriate based on current research.

Editor's note: Same-sex marriage was legalised in Australia three months after publication of this article, on 9 December 2017, after 61.6 per cent of respondents to a national postal survey voted 'Yes' to legalisation.

Why some kids can't spell and why spelling tests won't help

Misty Adoniou
Senior Lecturer in Language, Literacy and TESL, University of Canberra

25 November 2013

A couple of years ago, early one morning, I received an SMS advising 'resadents to stay indoors because of a nearby insadent'. I was shocked by the spelling, as much as the message. Surely, I thought, if it was a real message then the spelling would be correct.

Spelling matters. In a text message from a friend teeing up a night out, 'c u at 8' is fine – but in an emergency warning text from a government agency, I expect the spelling to be standard. But why is it that some people struggle with standard spelling?

Spelling remains the most relentlessly tested of all the literacy skills, but it is the least taught.

Sending a list of words home on Monday to be tested on Friday is not teaching. Nor is getting children to write their spelling words out ten times, even if they have to do it in rainbow colours.

Looking, covering, writing and checking does not teach spelling. Looking for little words inside other words and doing word searches are just time fillers. And writing your 'spelling' words in spirals or backwards is just plain stupid.

And yet, this is a good summary of most of the spelling programs in schools today.

So, what should spelling teaching look like?

Finding meaning

Children should know the meanings of the words they spell and, as logical as that sounds, ask a child in your life what this week's spelling words mean, and you might be surprised by their answers.

If spelling words are simply strings of letters to be learned by heart with no meaning attached and no investigation of how those words are constructed, then we are simply assigning our children a task equivalent to learning ten random seven-digit PINs each week.

That is not only very, very hard, it's pointless.

More than sounds

English is an alphabetic language; we use letters to write words. But it is not a phonetic language: there is no simple match between sounds and letters.

We have twenty-six letters, but we have around forty-four sounds (it's not easy to be precise, as different accents produce different sounds) and several hundred ways to write those sounds.

So, while sounds – or phonics – are important in learning to spell, they are insufficient. When the only tool we give young children for spelling is to 'sound it out', we are making a phonological promise to them that English simply cannot keep.

How words make their meanings

Sounds are important in learning to spell, but just as important are the morphemes in words. Morphemes are the meaningful parts of words. For example, 'jumped' has two morphemes – 'jump' and 'ed'. 'Jump' is easily recognised as meaningful, but 'ed' is also meaningful because it tells us that the jump happened in the past.

Young spellers who are relying on the phonological promise given to them in their early years of schooling typically spell 'jumped' as 'jumt'.

When attempting to spell a word, the first question we should teach children to ask is not 'What sounds can I hear?' but 'What does this word mean?'. This gives important information, which helps enormously with the spelling of the word.

In the example of 'jumt', it brings us back to the base word 'jump'; where the sound of 'p' can now be heard, and the past marker 'ed', rather than the sound 't', which we hear when we say the word.

Consider the author of the emergency text message at the beginning of this article as they pondered which of the many plausible letters they could use for the sound they could hear in 'res - uh - dent'.

If they had asked themselves first, 'What does this word mean?', the answer would have been people who 'reside', and then they would have heard the answer to their phonological dilemma.

Where words come from

English has a fascinating and constantly evolving history. Our words, and their spellings, come from many languages. Often we have kept the spellings from the original languages, while applying our own pronunciation.

As a result, only about 12 per cent of words in English are spelled the way they sound. But that doesn't mean spelling is inexplicable, and therefore only learned by rote – it means that teaching spelling becomes a fascinating exploration of the remarkable history of the language: etymology.

Some may think etymology is the sole province of older and experienced learners, but it's not.

Young children are incredibly responsive to stories about words, and these understandings about words are key to building their spelling skills, but also to building their vocabulary.

Yet, poor spellers and young spellers are rarely given these additional tools to understand how words work and too often poor spellers are relegated to simply doing more phonics work.

Teaching – not testing

The only people who benefit from spelling tests are those who do well on them – and the benefit is to their self-esteem rather than their spelling ability. They were already good spellers.

The people who don't benefit from spelling tests are those who are poor at spelling. They struggled with spelling before the test, and they still struggle after the test. Testing is not teaching.

Parents and teachers should consider these questions as they reflect on the ways in which spelling is approached in their school.

Are all children learning to love words from their very first years at school? Are they being fascinated by stories about where words come from and what those stories tell us about the spelling of those words?

Are they being excited by breaking the code, figuring how words are making their meanings and thrilled to find that what they've learned about one word helps them solve another word?

Put simply – is spelling your child's favourite subject?

If the answer is no, then something needs to be done about the teaching.

Sorry, men, there's no such thing as 'dirt blindness' – you just need to do more housework

Leah Ruppanner
Senior Lecturer in Sociology, University of Melbourne
Brendan Churchill
Research Fellow in Sociology, University of Melbourne

6 August 2018

The problem with housework is that it is never-ending drudgery. As soon as the floor is cleaned, the dog throws up, the kids spill slime ingredients into the wood grain, and the tradie walks through the house with well-oiled work boots. And the cycle begins again.

The Danish use the word *hygge* to describe the feeling of cosiness, warmth and comfort that a well-kept house is supposed to provide. Yet, creating this pleasant environment requires work and, unfortunately, the bulk of that work is done by women.

Findings from the latest Household, Income and Labour Dynamics in Australia (HILDA) report show Australian men have increased their housework time by fifty-five minutes and women have reduced theirs by two-and-a-half hours per week. So, the gender gap in housework is narrowing.

Yet, women still do seven hours more housework per week than men. Do women just have a love of cleaning that men do not share? Or are men 'dirt blind' – unable to see the mess as it emerges and takes over the sofa?

Fortunately for humankind, the answer to both of these questions is no. Let's unpack some of the main reasons why women's housework share remains larger than men's, and offer solutions to tidy up this gendered mess.

Men and 'dirt blindness' is a furphy

While attitudes towards gender roles have become less traditional, there are still gendered expectations about cleanliness of the home and children.

Any dirt, mess or failure to provide clean, immaculately dressed and polite children to the world is most often a judgement against women – a sure sign of bad mothering. Inherent in this assumption is the idea that men don't see mess or are oblivious to the cleaning and mental work associated with ensuring the household runs properly.

Even when housework is outsourced, women are more often responsible for organising and paying the cleaner or hitting the button on the full dishwasher or robot vacuum.

What's more, the types of domestic work that are outsourced are usually the work often done by men, such as gardening or household maintenance. Therefore, the benefit of domestic outsourcing is usually marginal for women.

Because of men's lack of desire to twirl a brush around the toilet bowl, or their general lack of worry about having a clean house, we tend to think of them as being 'dirt blind'. But really it's because men aren't penalised for messiness in the same way women are.

For women, cleanliness in the family home is a further extension of prevailing social norms dictating they must be clean, hairless, perfumed and pretty. In this regard, doing housework is a way for women to 'perform' their gender.

Men not doing housework also fits with long-held ideas about men and dirt that begin with boys and the outdoors. Thus, keeping house is as much about gendered expectations as it is about actual dirt. Men do see dirt, but they aren't told from a young age that leaving a mess makes them bad men.

Women's resources are discounted

In 2017, Australian women earned 87 cents for every dollar earned by a man. The gender pay gap in Australia has hovered between 15 per cent and 19 per cent for the past two decades.

Mothers, regardless of their profession, earn less than fathers, indicating that gender discrimination, rather than competence or occupational type, explains these gaps. (See 'Has the price of motherhood declined over time? A cross-cohort comparison of the motherhood wage penalty' by Sarah Avellar and Pamela J Smock.)

The gap in earnings is important, as having more money gives women more power – including to outsource housework. Studies show women are more likely than men to use their earnings to outsource housework. Women who are equal earners to men report the most equal housework divisions. (See 'Opting out and buying out: Wives' earnings and housework time' by Alexandra Killewald.)

Yet, when women start to earn more than their husbands, their earnings are less effective than men's in getting their husbands to increase their housework share. Housework scholarship has long documented that women who earn more than their male partners spend more, not less, time in housework than women whose earnings equal men's. (See 'Economic dependency, gender, and the division of labor at home' by Julie Brines.)

In other words, as women's earnings exceed men's, these earnings become a less valuable bargaining tool within a relationship. A recent study from the US census shows women who earn more than their partners under-report their own and overstate their husbands' earnings. (See 'Manning up and womaning down: How husbands and wives report their earnings when she earns more' by Marta Murray-Close and Misty L Heggeness.)

So, arguments that women can use their higher earnings to negotiate for husbands' greater housework contributions do not hold true.

Closing the gap in housework

A recent study about housework posed a dire warning: at the current pace, it will take thirty years for the gender gap in housework to close. (See 'Who is doing what on the homefront?' by Dr Inga Lass.) This is unlikely to eventuate unless we dramatically rethink the way men and women organise their work and family lives in Australia.

But there are a few ways forward. First, governments can provide help in the form of subsidies to hire cleaners or buy prepared meals, to help families reduce their housework burden.

The Swedes have instituted a tax credit for housework to help reduce the family's load and to bring this type of black-market labour into the light. (See 'Tax deductions for domestic service work, Sweden'.)

The second is for women to reduce their housework to similar levels as men. Based on current estimates, this means women will contribute fifty-five minutes per week. We could call this a housework strike – a way to draw attention to the unseen housework women do and to encourage men's equal contribution. This will require women to become 'dirt blind' and hold out until a crisis point is reached, such as everyone in the house running out of clean underwear.

However, women still do more childcare than men, so this won't solve all of women's domestic woes. The final solution is for men to see housework for what it is – drudgery we all have to do in order to achieve *hygge*. Men have heeded the call to increase their time with children – now a housework revolution is necessary for us all to relax.

PART II

Powerful stories

I was stabbed fourteen times at the hospital where I work. I survived, but not everyone is so lucky

Michael Wong
Neurosurgeon and Spinal Surgeon, University of Melbourne

23 August 2017

The attacker struck in the foyer of Melbourne's Footscray Hospital on an otherwise ordinary Tuesday morning.

I'd just arrived, and had my mobile phone out to ring my registrar to ask whether I had time to nick up to the wards and see my patients, or whether I needed to go straight to the outpatient clinic.

At first I thought I'd been pushed in the back. Then I slipped on my own blood and fell to the floor. I was being stabbed, over and over again. I remember turning my head so a blow coming at my eye instead landed on my skull. Being a neurosurgeon, I could all too easily picture the blade piercing my brain through the eye socket.

I remember people yelling, and the tug on my clothing as I was dragged along the floor through a set of double doors to safety, and along the corridors to Emergency, leaving a trail of blood.

The full story of my rescue and the incredible bravery and people behind it – including nurses, an intern, a hospital technician and a leukaemia patient – only emerged much later.

I remember looking at my arms and hands; there were deep cuts. I remember being aware that I was breathless and trying to slow my breathing – not knowing I had a punctured lung. I remember the look of absolute horror on my registrar's face, as I was wheeled past him on a hospital trolley on my way to surgery.

I remember asking someone to call my wife.

I remember the pain of being prepped for surgery, the sting of antiseptics on open wounds, and asking the anaesthetist why they couldn't put me to sleep first. (They didn't tell me it was for fear that I would go into arrest, and they wanted to wait until the full medical team was assembled.)

Hazily, I remember waking with a tube in my throat and seeing my wife – then things fade out until I woke to the moment of truth.

I was lucky

It was 2 am and I was alone, in a hospital bed. I knew where I was and what had happened. The big question, my big fear, was that I might have had a stroke as a result of the attack. I moved one side of my body, and then the other. Both sides worked. It was then that I felt I would be okay in the end.

All up, I was stabbed fourteen times. But I was lucky.

I was fortunate that, instead of being bystanders, brave people intervened to get me away from my attacker. The surgical team did an incredible job of stitching me back together, with a cardio-thoracic surgeon removing part of my lung to stem the bleeding, and three plastic surgeons mending severed tendons and muscles in my arms and hands.

I was also lucky to have a supportive family who helped me through the process of recovery.

My arms and hands were in splints for six weeks. I couldn't eat without help, or get dressed. I couldn't wipe my own backside – at times, I had my eight-year-old son helping me in the bathroom. If that's not humbling, I don't know what is.

Ironically, there was a part of me that was pleased to have some time off from the constant pressure to work more and more hours in the resource-constrained public hospital system. At the time of my recovery, MH370 went missing, and I watched hours and hours of coverage on TV.

When the splints came off, I was fortunate to have a hand therapist who worked with me over the next twelve months to enable me to regain strength and movement.

I was also lucky to be able to recover fully and return to work.

And I've been lucky that I don't seem to have been left psychologically scarred – other than disliking crowded areas in hospitals, and people walking behind me.

People ask how I can have escaped psychological damage. I think it's partly because in my career I've seen a lot of bad things – four-year-olds with malignant brain tumours, young people smashed to pieces.

I know bad things happen to good people, so I didn't waste time asking *why*, instead focusing on *what* I needed to do to recover.

If anything, my experience has made me a better doctor – not from a technical perspective, but in terms of having a deeper understanding of how it feels to be a patient, including the inconvenience and loss of control, the fear and pain. I came to understand that the essence of good care was time.

For the most part, I've compartmentalised the attack and put it away, and that seems to work for me.

Protecting staff

I don't enjoy revisiting the attack, but as someone fortunate enough to have survived, I speak out about my experiences to campaign for better hospital security – most recently, in the wake of a fatal one punch assault on Melbourne cardiothoracic surgeon Dr Patrick Pritzwald-Stegmann.

My attacker was mentally unwell. People ask me if 'the way forward' is better mental health care. While that would be welcome, the solutions I'm calling for are simpler.

First, busy public areas of hospitals should have trained security guards in them. You can't have security guards everywhere, but I think it's realistic to expect they can be stationed in hospital foyers and outpatient clinics – as well as emergency departments.

Second, fewer areas of hospitals should be public. All wards should be accessible only via swipe card access in the same way surgical theatres are protected today.

Third, hospitals should have secure entries for staff.

Hospital staff also need to play their part by taking the time to report violent incidents – ideally, on easy-to-use, streamlined report forms.

Management need to take the issue seriously – there's a good business case for investments that reduce occupational violence. Dealing with violent patients or bystanders wastes staff time. If staff are injured, they may need to take time off work for treatment. Indirectly, occupational violence contributes to stress that can lead to burnout, psychological damage and employee turnover. There are also issues of legal liability.

An analysis by *The Age* of Victorian hospital annual reports in 2015–16 found there were 8627 violent incidents reported – almost one an hour – with 1166 resulting injuries. While it is commendable annual reports must include this data (and other states should follow suit), the true number is probably far higher, due to under-reporting.

In the past year, in my own practice, I've operated on two hospital employees suffering severe back pain as a result of occupational violence at the hands of patients. It's not just physical pain they suffered but emotional trauma. I had a grown man weeping in my rooms.

In the wake of the attack on Dr Pritzwald-Stegmann, but before his death, the Victorian government hit the headlines with a new advertising campaign and a doubling of funding (to A$40 million) to the Health Service Violence Prevention Fund. Hospital administrators will be able to apply for funding for projects they believe will have the most impact.

While any funding is good funding, and gift horses shouldn't be looked in the mouth, this system relies on hospital administrators to be proactive and accurately judge the merits of competing proposals. Unfortunately, there are no guarantees the money will be spent to achieve the greatest possible impact across all public hospitals.

I did not know him personally, but clearly Patrick was doing valuable, lifesaving work for the Australian community when he was cut down in his prime. And, of course, he wasn't just a surgeon but a husband and father too. It's a senseless loss that no family should have to endure, and one that tragically further underlines the importance of getting hospital security right.

Chernobyl has become a refuge for wildlife thirty-three years after the nuclear accident

Germán Orizaola
Researcher at the Ramón y Cajal Program, Universidad de Oviedo

8 May 2019

Reactor number four of the Chernobyl Nuclear Power Plant suffered an explosion during a technical test on 26 April 1986. As a result of the accident, in the then Soviet Union, more than 400 times more radiation was emitted than was released by the atomic bomb dropped on Hiroshima, Japan, in 1945. It remains the largest nuclear accident in history.

Decontamination work began immediately after the accident. An exclusion zone was created around the plant, and more than 350,000 people were evacuated from the area. They never returned; and severe restrictions on permanent human settlement are still in place today.

The accident had a major impact on the human population. Although there are not clear figures, the physical loss of human lives and physiological consequences were huge. Estimates of the number of human fatalities vary wildly.

The initial impact on the environment was also important. One of the areas more heavily affected by the radiation was the pine forest near the plant, known since then as the 'Red Forest'. This area received the highest doses of radiation, the pine trees died instantly and all the leaves turned red. Few animals survived the highest radiation levels.

Therefore, after the accident it was assumed that the area would permanently become a desert. Considering the long time that some radioactive compounds take to decompose and disappear from the environment, the forecast was that the area would remain devoid of wildlife for centuries.

Chernobyl wildlife today

But today, thirty-three years after the accident, the Chernobyl exclusion zone, which covers an area now in Ukraine and Belarus, is inhabited by brown bears, bisons, wolves, lynxes, Przewalski's horses, and more than 200 bird species, among other animals.

In March 2019, most of the main research groups working with Chernobyl wildlife met in Portsmouth, England. About thirty of us researchers from the United Kingdom, Ireland, France, Belgium, Norway, Spain and Ukraine presented the latest results of our work. These studies included work on big mammals, nesting birds, amphibians, fish, bumblebees, earthworms, bacteria and leaf litter decomposition.

These studies showed that, at present, the area hosts great biodiversity. In addition, they confirmed the general lack of big negative effects of current radiation levels on the animal and plant populations in Chernobyl. All the studied groups maintain stable and viable populations inside the exclusion zone.

A clear example of the diversity of wildlife in the area is given by the TREE project (TRansfer-Exposure-Effects, led by Nick Beresford of the UK Centre for Ecology and Hydrology). As part of this project, motion detection cameras were installed for several years in different areas of the exclusion zone. The photos recorded by these cameras reveal the presence of abundant fauna at all levels of radiation. These cameras recorded the first observation of brown bears and European bison inside the Ukrainian side of the zone, as well as the increase in the number of wolves and Przewalski's horses.

European bison (*Bison bonasus*), boreal lynx (*Lynx lynx*), moose (*Alces alces*) and brown bear (*Ursus arctos*) photographed inside the Chernobyl exclusion zone, Ukraine. (Proyecto TREE/Sergey Gaschack)

Our own work with the amphibians of Chernobyl has also detected abundant populations across the exclusion zone, even on the more contaminated areas. Furthermore, we have also found signs that could represent adaptive responses to life with radiation. For instance, frogs within the exclusion zone are darker than frogs living outside it, which is a possible defence against radiation.

Studies have also detected some negative effects of radiation at an individual level. For example, some insects seem to have a shorter life span and are more affected by parasites in areas of high radiation. Some birds also have higher levels of albinism, as well as physiological and genetic alterations when living in highly contaminated localities. But these effects don't seem to have an impact on the maintenance of wildlife population in the area.

The general absence of negative effects from radiation on Chernobyl wildlife can be a consequence of several factors.

First, wildlife could be much more resistant to radiation than previously thought. Another possibility is that some organisms could be starting to show adaptive responses that would allow them to cope with radiation and live inside the exclusion zone without harm. In addition, the absence of humans inside the exclusion zone could be favouring many species – big mammals, in particular.

That final option would suggest that the pressures generated by human activities would be more negative for wildlife in the medium term than a nuclear accident – a quite revealing vision of the human impact on the natural environment.

The future of Chernobyl

In 2016 the Ukrainian part of the exclusion zone was declared a radiological and environmental biosphere reserve by the national government.

Over the years, Chernobyl has also become an excellent natural laboratory for the study of evolutionary processes in extreme environments. This is something that could prove valuable, given the rapid environmental changes experienced worldwide.

At present, several projects are trying to resume human activities in the area. Tourism has flourished in Chernobyl, with more than 70,000 visitors in 2018. There are also plans for developing solar power plants in the area, and for expanding forestry work. Last year, there was even an art installation and techno party inside the abandoned city of Prypiat.

Over the past thirty-three years, Chernobyl has gone from being considered a potential permanent desert to being an area of high interest for biodiversity conservation.

It may sound strange, but now we need to work to maintain the integrity of the exclusion zone as a nature reserve if we want to guarantee that Chernobyl will remain a refuge for wildlife.

Magpies can form friendships with people – here's how

Gisela Kaplan
Emeritus Professor in Animal Behaviour, University of New England

3 October 2017

Can one form a friendship with a magpie – even when adult males are protecting their nests during the swooping season? The short answer is 'Yes, one can' – although science has just begun to provide feasible explanations for friendship in animals, let alone for cross-species friendships between humans and wild birds.

Ravens and magpies are known to form powerful allegiances among themselves. In fact, Australia is thought to be a hotspot for cooperative behaviour in birds worldwide. They like to stick together with family and mates, in the good old Australian way.

Of course, many bird species may readily come to a feeding table and become tame enough to take food from our hand, but this isn't really 'friendship'. However, there is evidence that, remarkably, free-living magpies can forge lasting relationships with people, even without depending on us for food or shelter.

When magpies are permanently ensconced on human property, they are also far less likely to swoop the people who live there. Over 80 per cent of all successfully breeding magpies live near human houses, which means the vast majority of people, in fact, never get swooped. And since magpies can live between twenty-five and thirty years and are territorial, they can develop lifelong friendships with humans. This bond can extend to trusting certain people around their offspring.

A key reason why friendships with magpies are possible is that we now know they are able to recognise and remember individual human faces for many years. They can learn which nearby humans do not constitute a risk. They will remember someone who was good to them; equally, they remember negative encounters.

Why become friends?

Magpies that actively form friendships with people make this investment (from their point of view) for good reason. Properties suitable for magpies are hard to come by and the competition is fierce. Most magpies will not secure a territory – let alone breed – until they are at least five years old. In fact, only about 14 per cent of adult magpies ever succeed in breeding. And, based on extensive magpie population research conducted by biologist and ornithologist Robert Carrick in the 1970s, even if they breed successfully every single year, they may successfully raise only seven to eleven chicks to adulthood and breeding in a lifetime. There is a lot at stake with every magpie clutch.

The difference between simply not swooping someone and a real friendship manifests in several ways. When magpies have formed an attachment, they will often show their trust, for example, by formally introducing their offspring. They may allow their chicks to play near people, not fly away when a resident human is approaching, and actually approach or roost near a human.

In rare cases, they may even join in human activity. For example, magpies have helped me garden by walking in parallel to my weeding activity and displacing soil as I did. One magpie always perched on my kitchen windowsill, looking in and watching my every move.

On one extraordinary occasion, an adult female magpie gingerly entered my house on foot, and hopped over to my desk, where I was sitting. She watched me type on the keyboard and even looked at the screen. I had to get up to take a phone call, and when I returned, the magpie had taken up a position at my keyboard; she pecked the keys gently and then looked at the 'results' on screen.

The bird was curious about everything I did. She also wanted to play with me, and found my shoelaces particularly attractive, pulling them and then running away a little, only to return for another go.

Importantly, it was the bird (not hand-raised but a free-living adult female) that had begun to take the initiative and had chosen to socially interact. Such behaviour, as research – particularly in primates – has shown, is affiliative, and part of the basis of social bonds and friendships.

Risky business

If magpies can be so good with humans, how can one explain their swooping at people (even if it is only for a few weeks in the year)? It's worth bearing in mind that swooping magpies (invariably males on guard duty) do not act in aggression or anger but as nest defenders. The strategy they choose is based on risk assessment.

A risk is posed by someone who is unknown and was not present at the time of nest building, which, unfortunately, is often the case in parks and other public places. That person is then classified as a territorial intruder and thus a potential risk to the male's brood. At this point, the male guarding the brooding female is obliged to perform a warning swoop, literally asking a person to step away from the nest area.

If warnings are ignored, the adult male may try to conduct a near contact swoop aimed at the head (the magpie can break its own neck if it makes contact, so it is a strategy of last resort). Magpie swooping is generally a defensive action taken when someone unknown approaches who the magpie believes intends harm. It is not an arbitrary attack.

When I was swooped for the first time in a public place, I slowly walked over to the other side of the road. Importantly, I allowed the male to study my face and appearance from a safe distance, so he could remember me in future, a useful strategy, given magpies' memory for human faces. Taking a piece of mince to him, or taking a wide berth around the bird's nest, may eventually convince the nervous magpie that he does not need to deter this individual anymore because she or he poses little or no risk; and, who knows, may even become a friend in future.

A sure way of escalating conflict is to fence them with an umbrella or any other device, or to run away at high speed. This human approach may well confirm for the magpie that the person is dangerous and needs to be fought with every available strategy.

In dealing with magpies, as in global politics, de-escalating a perceived conflict is usually the best strategy.

'They put a few coins in your hands to drop a baby in you' – 265 stories of Haitian children abandoned by UN fathers

Sabine Lee
Professor in Modern History, University of Birmingham

Susan Bartels
Clinician-Scientist, Queen's University, Ontario

18 December 2019

Marie* was fourteen years old and enrolled in a Christian school when she met and became involved with Miguel, a Brazilian soldier working in Haiti as a UN peacekeeper. When she told him she was pregnant with his baby, Miguel said he would help her with the child. But, instead, he returned to Brazil. Marie wrote to him on Facebook but he never responded.

After learning she was pregnant, Marie's father forced her to leave the family home and she went to live with her sister. Her child is now four and Marie has yet to receive any support from the Brazilian military, an NGO, the UN or the Haitian state. Marie provides what she can for her son but she cannot afford to send him to school. She works for an hourly wage of 25 gourde (around US 26 cents) so that she and her son can eat. But she needs help with housing and paying for school fees.

Sadly, Marie's experience is far from unique. In the summer of 2017, our research team interviewed approximately 2500 Haitians about the experiences of local women and girls living in communities that host peace support operations. Of those, 265 told stories that featured children fathered by UN personnel. That 10 per cent of those interviewed mentioned such children highlights just how common such stories really are.

The narratives reveal how girls as young as eleven were sexually abused and impregnated by peacekeepers and then, as one man put it, 'left in misery' to raise their children alone, often because the fathers are repatriated once the pregnancy becomes known. Mothers such as Marie are then left to raise the children in settings of extreme poverty and disadvantage, with most receiving no assistance.

Mired in controversy

The UN Stabilization Mission in Haiti (MINUSTAH) – the longest-running mission by the organisation in the country (2004–17) – was originally mandated to assist local Haitian institutions in a context of political instability and organised crime. Its mandate was then extended due to natural disasters: most notably, an earthquake in 2010 and Hurricane Matthew in 2016, both of which added to the volatility of the political situation in the country. After thirteen years of operation, MINUSTAH closed in October 2017, transitioning to the smaller UN Mission for Justice Support in Haiti (MINUJUSTH).

MINUSTAH is one of the most controversial UN missions ever. It has been the focus of extensive allegations of sexual exploitation and abuse. A shocking number of uniformed and non-uniformed peacekeeping personnel have been linked to human rights abuses, including sexual exploitation, rape and even unlawful deaths. (For the purposes of this article, we use MINUSTAH personnel, agents, and peacekeepers interchangeably to refer to uniformed and non-uniformed foreign staff associated with MINUSTAH.)

With regard to public health, it is undisputed, and now officially recognised by the UN, that peacekeepers also inadvertently introduced cholera to Haiti. More than 800,000 Haitians are known to have sought medical attention for cholera and at least 10,000 have died from the disease.

Various media organisations have reported that minors were offered food and small amounts of cash to have sex with UN personnel, and MINUSTAH was linked to a sex ring that operated in Haiti with seeming impunity: allegedly, at least 134 Sri Lankan peacekeepers exploited nine children in a sex ring from 2004 to 2007. As a result of this story, reported by the Associated Press in 2017, MINUSTAH became a classic example of a lack of appropriate response to allegations of sexual abuse. In the wake of this report, 114 peacekeepers were returned to Sri Lanka, but none were ever prosecuted or charged after repatriation.

Extensive research has demonstrated that children born of war are often raised in single-parent families in precarious economic post-conflict settings. The association with the (absent) foreign father, along with birth out of wedlock, often result in stigma and discrimination for the children.

Yet, little is known about the impact of being a mixed-race child fathered by peacekeepers. Even less is known about the experiences of the so-called 'Petit MINUSTAH', or Haitian-born children of foreign UN peacekeepers. This is one of the reasons we set out to bring to light the stories of those affected by the UN mission.

Our study

We collected stories by asking participants to tell us what it's like to be a woman or girl living in a community that hosts a peacekeeping mission. We audio-recorded the resulting stories, and then participants interpreted their experiences by responding to a series of pre-defined questions. This allowed us to better understand the circumstances and consequences of their interactions with peacekeepers.

Participants could share any story they chose, about anyone, and were not prompted in any way to talk about sexual abuse or exploitation.

Narratives were captured by trained Haitian research assistants in the communities surrounding ten UN bases in Haiti in the summer of 2017. About 2500 Haitians were asked about the experiences of local women and girls living in communities that host peace support operations. A variety of positive and negative experiences were captured, but 265 (10 per cent) of all stories were about peacekeeper-fathered children. This is particularly noteworthy since the survey did not ask about sexual relations with peacekeepers or about children conceived through such relations.

This would suggest not only that sexual abuse and exploitation by UN peacekeeping personnel is not rare, but also, as one Port-Salut research participant said in her own words: 'There are many young women who have children with the MINUSTAH.' This was echoed by a man in Saint-Marc, who told us: 'MINUSTAH gave us many children without fathers.'

Some stories were first person, shared by those who had given birth to children fathered by UN personnel; while other stories were told by family members, friends or neighbours about women and girls raising children fathered by peacekeepers. To the best of our knowledge, these stories make up the first empirical research to bring forth the voices of families affected by sexual exploitation and abuse by UN peacekeepers.

Sex for one meal

Some sexual encounters between local women and girls and UN peacekeeping personnel were described as sexual violence. For instance, a male community member in Cité Soleil recounted: 'All day, I heard women who are complaining about the sexual violence that MINUSTAH did to them. And they had given them AIDS through sexual violence. There are also some of them who are pregnant.'

There were not only stories of women and girls being sexually assaulted by MINUSTAH but also of men and boys being similarly abused. But in our research, sexual assault was in the minority of reported sexual encounters. Instead, our data highlighted a much more pervasive problem, albeit one that has been reported less in the media – transactional sex with UN personnel.

One married man from Cité Soleil described a common pattern in which women received small amounts of money in exchange for sex:

'They come, they sleep with the women, they take their pleasures with them, they leave children in their hands, give them 500 gourdes.'

In other cases of transactional sex, women and girls received food in exchange for having sex with members of MINUSTAH, highlighting the extreme poverty that contributes to these sexual encounters. One male community member in Port-Salut reported: 'They had sex with the girls not even for money, it's just for food, for one meal.'

Evolving relationships

Another narrative that has received far less attention in previous reports is how consensual sexual relations between members of MINUSTAH and local women evolve. In some instances, these were casual dating relationships that resulted in a pregnancy, as was the case in this story, shared by a man in Port-Salut: 'I had a sister who was dating a MINUSTAH soldier. My whole family knew about it, my mother as well as other people. She became pregnant ... Ever since, my sister's life is a mess.'

Other relationships were described as being more committed and loving, such as in this story shared by a woman in Cité Soleil, who said: 'I was living in Cité Soleil and I was in a love relationship with a MINUSTAH. I became pregnant from him.'

We found that intimate relations with fair-skinned peacekeepers and having fair-skinned children were sometimes perceived as desirable. A woman in Léogâne described 'rumours' about girls having relationships with MINUSTAH and having their children because they 'wanted these children to be beautiful'.

Regardless of whether the relationship was consensual or transactional in nature, particular patterns were noted in how and where the interactions took place. For instance, meeting on the beach or in a hotel was common, as in this story shared by a woman in Cité Soleil, about a friend of hers: 'He used to go to the beach with her, now the white man paid for a hotel for her, the white man goes to the hotel with her, he comes to have sex with her.'

Also of great concern is that many of the mothers giving birth to and raising children fathered by UN peacekeepers were themselves adolescents and not old enough to give consent for sex. One woman in Cité Soleil told us: 'I see a series of females 12 and 13 years old here. MINUSTAH impregnated and left them in misery with babies in their hands. The person has already had to manage a stressful, miserable life.'

Abandonment

Most shared stories indicated that after learning of a resultant pregnancy, the MINUSTAH personnel were repatriated by the UN. One woman in Port-Salut told us: 'One of my sisters gave birth to a child of the MINUSTAH. My sister had a baby with him because she met him, fell in love with him, he took care of her, but you know, they were sent away. That is why he stopped sending her things.'

A male participant in Hinche described a similar experience of a girl he knew, saying: 'She was pregnant from a soldier of the MINUSTAH ... [He] was moved from his station and left his post and was never seen again.'

After the departure of the peacekeeper fathers, most young women were alone, trying to raise the children in extreme poverty. Some, although certainly not all, described being fortunate enough to receive support from their families.

In almost all cases, access to education was beyond the mother's or the family's means, as described by one woman in Port-Salut: 'I started to talk to him, then he told me he loved me and I agreed to date him. Three months later, I was pregnant, and in September he was sent to his country ... The child is growing up, and it's myself and my family that are struggling with him. I now have to send him to school. They put him out because I'm unable to pay for it.'

A man in Cap-Haïtien said: 'The soldiers destroy these young girls' futures by getting them pregnant with a couple of babies and abandoning them. Basically, these actions of the soldiers can have a negative impact on the society and on the country in general because these young girls could have been lawyers, doctors or anything that would have helped Haiti tomorrow ... Now some of them are walking in the street, or in the flea market and other places, with a basket over their head selling oranges, peppers, and other goods in order to raise children they have with the MINUSTAH soldiers.'

In a few extreme cases, community members described women and girls who were left with little option other than to engage in further sex with peacekeepers in order to provide for the MINUSTAH children they were already raising. A man in Port-au-Prince shared one example: 'He left her in misery because when he used to have sex with her it was for little money, now his term reaches its end, he goes and leaves her in misery, and then now she has to redo the same process so she can provide meals to her child, can't you understand.'

In the stories we collected, there were many requests for MINUSTAH and the Haitian authorities to help support these children. One man in Port-Salut stated his request very clearly: 'I would like to ask the head of MINUSTAH to take responsibility for the children of MINUSTAH members ... We are just doing what we can but you cannot raise children like this...'

Power and exploitation

Our research has underlined what is implied in much of the academic literature on peacekeeping economies – namely, that poverty is a key underlying factor contributing to sexual abuse and exploitation by peacekeeping forces.

In many cases, the power differential between foreign peacekeepers and local populations allows foreigners, knowingly or unknowingly, to exploit local women and girls. The prevalence of transactional sex in our data underscores the significance of the structural imbalances – peacekeepers have access to some of the resources that are desired or needed by the local population and so they are in a strong position to exchange those for sex.

While many of the stories cited above were collected in Port-Salut and Cité Soleil, similar narratives were shared across all interview sites in Haiti and the phenomena described are not unique to the Haitian context. Our preliminary work in the Democratic Republic of the Congo suggests a comparable situation.

In its zero-tolerance policy, the UN acknowledges the existence of socioeconomic and other power imbalances, and their potential to render 'intimacies' between peacekeepers and local women exploitative. In essence, the policy bans almost all sexual relations between peacekeepers and local women. In addition to suggesting that this blanket ban is ineffective, our data indicates that a more nuanced approach, with targeted training of UN personnel, is required, alongside tackling the impunity that still surrounds peacekeeper wrongdoing.

Another key finding is the need for more effective mechanisms allowing victims of sexual exploitation and abuse and their children (as well as children of consensual and non-exploitative relations) to access support. This could potentially break the socioeconomic downward spiral that traps victims – and, in particular, children – in circumstances of extreme economic hardship, perpetuating the cycle of poverty.

Child support

In January 2018, the Haitian-based Bureau des Avocats Internationaux (BAI) filed paternity suits in Haitian courts on behalf of ten children fathered by UN peacekeepers, with the aim of lobbying the UN to secure child support payments for those children. A year later, an open letter from the bureau to UN Victims' Rights Advocate Jane Connors betrays their frustration with the UN's lack of responsiveness and cooperation with the paternity suits, which 'has made it nearly impossible for our clients to obtain justice'.

Evidencing the UN's refusal to furnish results of DNA paternity tests that are vital to the mothers' cases, despite a Haitian court order compelling it to do so, the letter concluded that the UN was sending 'an alarming message of lack of respect for the Haitian judicial system and the rule of law'.

This raises questions regarding the UN's rhetoric about supporting the dignity and rights of those affected by sexual exploitation and abuse perpetrated by its peacekeepers. It also calls into question the effectiveness of interventions of the Office of the Victims' Rights Advocate, which exists to advocate for the rights of victims and to bring their needs to the forefront of the UN's fight against sexual exploitation and abuse.

Recommendations

The findings from our research have led us to make three key recommendations.

1. Training of UN personnel must include a cultural awareness aspect, to enhance understanding of the impact of power differentials in fragile peacekeeping economies, the perceived desirability of having a child fathered by a peacekeeper, and the socioeconomic consequences for a vulnerable woman being left with a peacekeeper-fathered child.

2. The UN practice of repatriating any UN personnel implicated in sexual exploitation or abuse must stop, as it has a double-negative consequence. First, it removes the alleged offender from any effective prosecution in the cases of alleged wrongdoing; and, second, it removes them from any jurisdiction within which the victim/child/mother of a child would have any chance of securing the appropriate financial support for the child.
3. The recent appointment of a Victims' Rights Advocate for those affected by sexual abuse and exploitation must be followed by a policy that will allow the advocate to tackle some of the injustices created by the exploitation and abuse at a structural level. At the same time, they must be allowed to become a powerful voice of the victims, speaking and working on their behalf within the UN and in collaboration with the host countries and the troop-contributing countries.

Many of the participants interviewed expressed similar sentiments regarding the need for recognition of, and support for, children fathered by UN peacekeepers in Haiti. One man said: 'I know a lot of young women, young girls, children, who are living with MINUSTAH children in their care ... I would like for them [the UN] to take responsibility, to take the initiative to look for and rejoin those young girls so that they can help them with the children.'

* *Names have been changed to protect participants' anonymity.*

Human trafficking and slavery still happen in Australia. This comic explains how

Jennifer Burn
Professor, Faculty of Law, University of Technology Sydney

Artwork by Wes Mountain
Multimedia Editor, The Conversation

12 June 2019

We might not want to believe it, but human trafficking and slavery happen in Australia. Slavery is not an historical artefact, but a tragic reality for millions of people around the world, including in Australia.

Recently, the term 'modern slavery' has been used to contrast contemporary forms of slavery with historical slavery such as that seen during the transatlantic slave trade.

In practice, modern slavery is an umbrella term that is often used to describe human trafficking, slavery and slavery-like practices, such as servitude, forced labour and forced marriage.

But slavery is timeless. It has always been about the commodification of the body of a man, woman or child, the theft of liberty and sometimes life.

Anti-Slavery Australia, at the University of Technology Sydney, started researching and assisting trafficked and enslaved people in Australia back in 2002. For over seventeen years, Anti-Slavery Australia has provided access to legal advice and assistance to hundreds of people who have experienced modern slavery.

In 2018 alone, Anti-Slavery Australia helped over 123 people who had been trafficked to or from Australia, or had faced slavery-like conditions while in Australia, including forced marriage, servitude and forced labour.

But this is just the tip of the iceberg. A 2019 report by the Australian Institute of Criminology ('Estimating the dark figure of human trafficking and slavery victimisation in Australia' by Samantha Lyneham et al.) estimates that only one in five victims are detected. This means the cases we see are likely to be a small proportion of the scale of trafficking and slavery in Australia.

Vulnerable people of any background or status can be cruelly exploited. Some groups, such as migrant workers or young people, are more vulnerable than others.

So, what does modern slavery look like in Australia?

Here are four real-world examples, with names of individuals and businesses changed, to explain the different kinds of exploitation seen by Anti-Slavery Australia and considered in Australian courts.

Slavery/domestic servitude

In Australian law, slavery is defined as 'the condition of a person over whom any or all of the powers attaching to the right of ownership are exercised, including where such a condition results from a debt or contract made by the person'.

Essentially, slavery is when a person is controlled as if they were mere property.

Mary was a 25-year-old woman from the Philippines.

Mary and her family lived in a single room, with no electricity or running water.

Mary left school when she was 13 years old to look after her younger siblings.
She was working in a sewing factory and earning $10 per week.

Mary's aunt arranged for her to get a job as a domestic worker in Australia.

Mary was told she would earn...
$800 a month

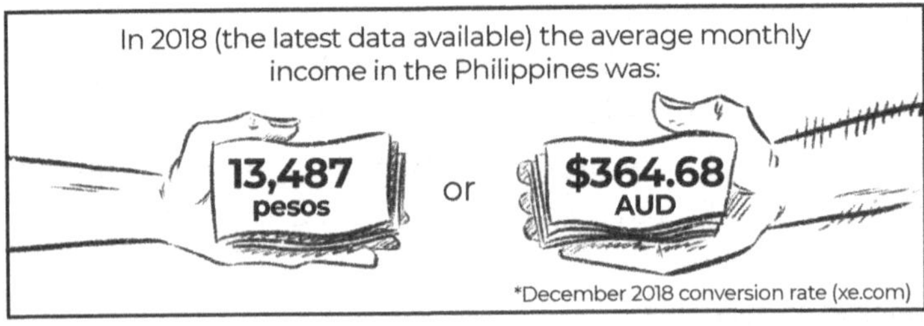
In 2018 (the latest data available) the average monthly income in the Philippines was:
13,487 pesos
or
$364.68 AUD
*December 2018 conversion rate (xe.com)

Mary didn't know much about Australia.
CABAYAN SA AUSTRALIA
And did not speak any English.

Mary's family encouraged her to go to Australia so she could support them better financially.

Mary arrived in Australia and was met by her new boss, Mr K, at the airport.
MARY
And her situation changed quickly after that.

Mary was forced to work from 6 am to 6 pm at Mr K and his wife's shop.
CHIPS
CHIPS

And then do the domestic work at Mr and Mrs K's house at night.

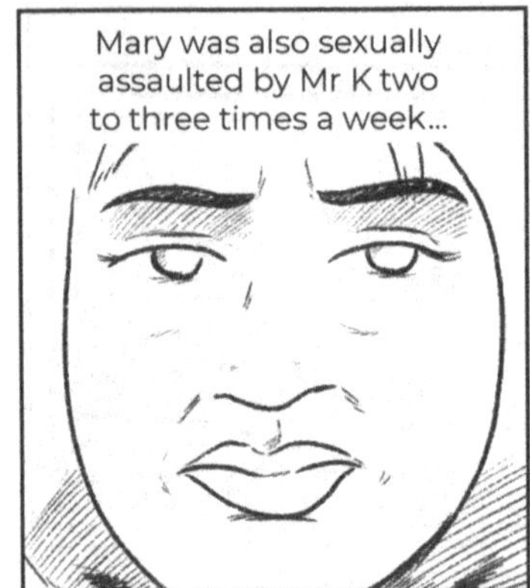

Eventually, with the help of one of Mr and Mrs K's family members, Mary was able to leave this situation.

This example is based on a case that ultimately led to Mr and Mrs K being found guilty of slavery offences and sentenced to eight years' and four years' imprisonment respectively.

Servitude

Servitude is when a person does not consider themselves to be free to stop working or leave their workplace, because of threats, coercion or deception; and the person is significantly deprived of personal freedom in their life outside of work.

and worked from 7.40 am to 9.30 pm every day.

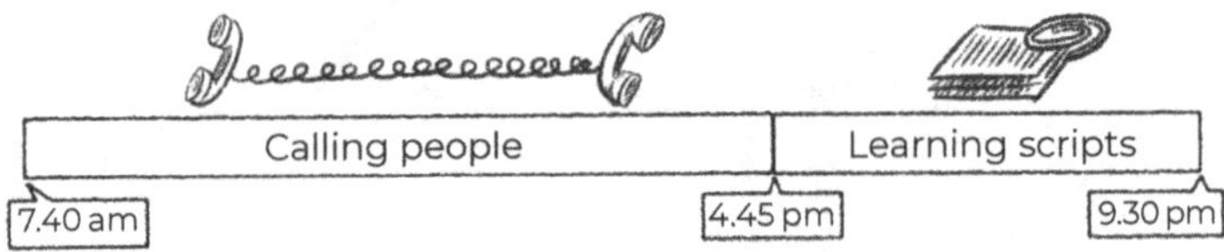

He and the others were told when they could...

Tom was not paid any wages for his work.

Eventually, Tom managed to escape from the house, flagged down a motorist and contacted the police, who found forty-nine other exploited people who had been coerced and controlled.

This example is based on a case that led to two people being found guilty of causing a person to enter into or remain in servitude, and sentenced to three years' and two-and-a-half years' imprisonment.

Forced marriage

A forced marriage is when a person is married without freely and fully consenting because of either coercion, threat or deception. It could also be because they're incapable of understanding the nature and effect of a marriage ceremony, possibly because of their age or mental capacity.

A forced marriage is different from an arranged marriage or a sham marriage. The main difference is that there is consent in arranged and sham marriages.

Jane was 17 and from a very traditional family.

She and her boyfriend had previously fled her parents, who had forbidden her from seeing him.
SYDNEY 25

After her parents begged her to come home, she agreed to travel with them to their country of birth.
They promised that she could marry her boyfriend when she returned.
DEPARTURE

On arrival, her parents took charge of her passport...
ARRIVALS

...and introduced her to a new suitor, who she was told she would marry.

Jane's parents threatened that her boyfriend's mother and sister would be kidnapped and harmed if she didn't go through with the marriage.

They also made threats directly to her boyfriend.

Jane's father also physically assaulted her on multiple occasions.
YOU WILL MARRY HIM!

Jane was eventually forced to get married while overseas.
She didn't even speak during the ceremony.

After the wedding, Jane was forced to assist with her new husband's Australian visa application.

Jane returned to Australia.
DEPARTURES

The Family Court of Australia found the marriage was not valid, because:
Her consent was not real because it was obtained by duress.

And that Jane had been physically and mentally coerced into marrying her husband.

The court found the marriage was not a real one.

Forced labour

Forced labour is when a person does not consider themselves free to stop working, or to leave their workplace, because of threats, coercion or deception.

John discovered he would have to...
work,
live
and sleep
in the restaurant.
ONIONS

At night, John was locked in the restaurant storeroom...
EMPLOYEES ONLY

...and had no key or any access to a bathroom until the owner returned in the morning.

John had limited food to eat.

And few breaks, as he worked from
8AM
MIDNIGHT

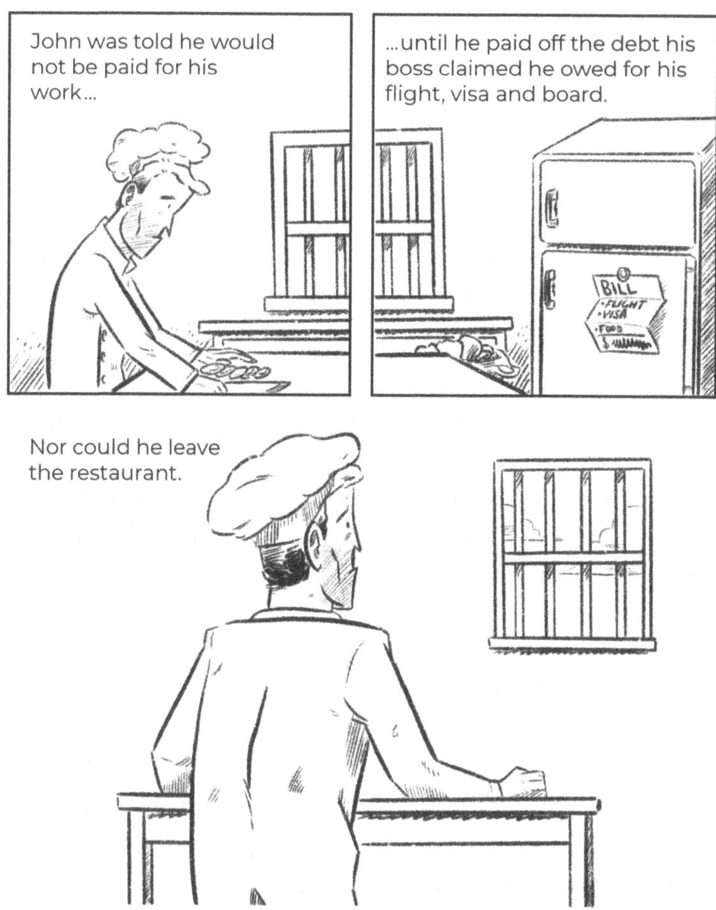

Eventually, John was able to get help, but he was in very poor health and died a few years later.

On the ending of a friendship

Kevin John Brophy
Emeritus Professor of Creative Writing, University of Melbourne

20 September 2019

'Friendship is an incomparable, immeasurable boon to me, and a source of life – not metaphorically but literally.'
—Simone Weil

About eight years ago, I went to dinner with a dear friend I had known for more than forty years. It would be the last time we would see each other and by the end of that evening I was deeply shaken. But more lasting and more unsettling than this has been the feeling of loss without his friendship. It was a sudden ending but it was also an ending that lasted for me well beyond that evening. I have worried since then about what kind of friend I am to my friends, and why a friendship can suddenly self-destruct while others can so unexpectedly bloom.

My friend and I were used to going to dinner together, though it had become an increasingly tricky matter for us. We had been seeing each other more infrequently, and our conversations had been tending towards repetition. I still enjoyed his passion for talk, his willingness to be puzzled by life's events, our comically growing list of minor ailments as we entered our sixties, and the old stories he fell back on – usually stories of his minor triumphs, such as the time his car burst into flame, was declared a write-off by the insurer and ended in an auction house, where he bought it back with part of the insurance payout and only minor repairs to be made. There were stories of his time as a barman in one of Melbourne's roughest pubs. I suppose in a lot of long-lasting friendships it is these repeated stories of the past that can fill the present so richly.

Nevertheless, both his opinions and mine seemed to have become too predictable. Even his desire to come up with the most unpredictable viewpoint on any problem was a routine I expected from him. Each of us knew the weaknesses in the other's thinking, and we had learned not to go too far with some topics, which were, of course, the most interesting and important ones.

He knew how politically correct I could be, and, shrewdly enough, he had no time for my self-righteousness, the predictability of my views on gender, race and climate. I understood this. He knew too that his fiercely independent thinking was often just the usual rant against greenies or lefties. Something had begun to fail in our friendship, but I could not properly perceive this or speak of it.

We were a contrasting pair. He was a big man with an aggressive edge to his gregarious nature, while I was lean, short and physically slight next to him, a much more reserved person altogether. I liked his size because big men have been protective figures in my life. At times when I felt threatened I would ask him to come with me to a meeting or a transaction, and just stand next to me in his big way. During one long period of trouble with our neighbours he would visit when the tension was high, to show his formidable presence and his solidarity with us.

I was always reading and knew how to talk books, while he was too restless to read much. He knew how to sing, bursting into song occasionally when we were together. He had been unable to work professionally since a breakdown that was both physical and mental. By contrast, I was working steadily, never quite as free with my time as he was with his.

Nearly two years before our last dinner together, his wife had suddenly left him. As it turned out, she had been planning her departure for some time, but when she went he was taken by surprise. I saw a more confused and fragile side of him during those months when we would meet and talk through how he was dealing with their counselling sessions, and then how the negotiations were proceeding over belongings and, finally, the family house. He was learning to live alone for the first time since he had been a young man, and was exploring what it might be like to seek out new relationships.

A safe haven

We had met when I was a first-year university student boarding at my grandmother's home in an inner Melbourne suburb. I was studying for a Bachelor of Arts, staying up through the nights, discovering literature, music, history, cask wine, dope, girls and ideas.

He lived in a flat a few doors away in a street behind my grandmother's place, and I remember it was the local parish youth group, or the remnants of one, that used to meet in his flat. In my friend's flat we would lie around the floor, half a dozen of us, drinking, flirting, arguing about religion or politics until the night was strung out in our heads, tight and thin and vibrating with possibilities. I loved that sudden intimate and intellectually rich contact with people my own age.

My friend and I started up a coffee lounge in an old disused shopfront as a meeting place for youth who would otherwise be on the street. I was the one who became immersed in the chaotic life of the place, as students, musicians, misfits, hopeful poets and petty criminals floated through the shop, while my friend kept his eye on the broader picture that involved real estate agents, local councils, supplies of coffee, and income and expenditure.

Perhaps the experience helped delay my own adulthood, allowing me time to try out a bohemian, communal alternative lifestyle that was so important to some of us in the early 1970s. My friend, though, was soon married. It was as if he had been living a parallel life outside our friendship, outside the youth group, coffee shop, jug band, drugs and misadventures of our project.

This did not break us up and, in fact, after his marriage he became another kind of friend. I was at times struggling to find some steady sense of myself. Sometimes in those years I would not be able to talk or even be near others, and I remember once when I felt like this I went to my newly married friend's home and asked if I could lie on the floor in the corner of their lounge room for a few days until I felt better.

They indulged me. I felt it was this haven that saved me then, giving me the time to recoup, and a sense that there was somewhere I could go where the world was safe and neutral.

In time, and more bumpily and uncertainly than my friend, I was with a partner, raising a family. He was often involved in our children's birthdays, other celebrations, our house-moving, and also just dropping in on family meals. It worked for us. I remember him lifting our cast-iron wood-burning stove into its place in our first renovated Brunswick cottage. He lived in a more sprawling home, near bushland on the edge of Melbourne, so one of my pleasures became the long cycling trips out to see him.

My partner and I were embraced by a local community, thanks to the childcare centre, kinders, schools and sport. Lasting friendships (for us and for our children) grew in their tentative, open-ended, slightly blindly feeling way. Through this decade and a half, though, the particular friendship with my songful friend held, perhaps to the surprise of both of us.

'Tolerating much, for the sake of best intentions'

In his thoroughly likeable 1993 book *Friendship: Being Ourselves with Others*, the political scientist Graham Little wrote, under the bright light of writings by Aristotle and Freud, that the purest kind of friendship 'welcomes the different ways people are alive to life and tolerates much in a friend for the sake of best intentions'.

Here, perhaps, is the closest I have seen to a definition of friendship at its best: a stance imbued with sympathy, interest and excitement directed at another, despite all that otherwise shows we are flawed and dangerous creatures.

On that evening, the evening of the last time we went out to dinner together, I did push my friend towards one of the topics we usually avoided. I had been wanting him to acknowledge, and even apologise for, his behaviour to some young women he had spoken to, I thought, lewdly and insultingly, nearly a year before at a party in my home. The women and those of us who had witnessed his behaviour felt continuing tension over his refusal to discuss the fact that he had wanted to speak so insultingly to them and then had done it in our home in front of us. For me, there was some element of betrayal, not only in the way he had behaved but in his continued refusal to discuss what had happened.

The women were drunk, he said, just as he had said the last time I tried to talk to him about this. They were wearing almost nothing, he said, and what he'd said to them was no more than they were expecting. My friend and I were sitting in a popular Thai restaurant on Sydney Road: metal chairs, plastic tables, concrete floor. It was noisy, packed with students, young couples and groups out for a cheap and tasty meal. A waitress had put menus, water and beer on our table while she waited for us to decide on our meals. Wanting to push finally past this impasse, I pointed out to him that the women had not insulted him, he had insulted them.

If that's the way you want it, he replied, and placed his hands on each side of the table, hurling it into the air, and walking out of the restaurant as the table, bottles, glasses, water and beer came clattering and smashing down around me. The whole restaurant fell silent. I could not move for some time. The waitress began mopping up the floor around me. Someone called out, 'Hey, are you all right?'

This was the last time I saw or heard from him. For many months, I thought of him every day, then slowly I thought of him less often, until now I can think of him more or less at will, and not find myself ashamed of the way I went for him in a conversation where I should have been, perhaps, more alive to whatever was troubling him.

Improvised, tentative

For some years after this, I felt I had to learn how to be myself without him. I have read articles and essays since then about how pitiful men can be at friendship. We are apparently too competitive, we base our friendships on common activities, which means we can avoid talking openly about our feelings and thoughts. I don't know about this 'male deficit model', as some sociologists call it, but I do know that the loss of this friendship took with it a big part of my shared personal history at that time. It dented my confidence in ever having properly known this man or understood our friendship – or in knowing how secure any friendship might be.

I was drawn to read and re-read Michel de Montaigne's gentle and strangely extreme essay *On Friendship*, where he was so certain that he knew with perfection what his friend would think and say and value. He wrote of his friend Étienne de Boétie, 'Not only did I know his mind as well as I knew my own but I would have entrusted myself to him with greater assurance than to myself.'

Against this perfection of understanding between friends, there is George Eliot's odd excursion into science fiction in her 1859 novel, *The Lifted Veil*. Her narrator, Latimer, finds he can perceive perfectly clearly the thoughts of all the people around him. He becomes disgusted and deeply disturbed by the petty self-interest he apparently discovers within everyone.

After forty years of shared history, there was not the disgust Eliot writes of, nor Montaigne's perfect union of mind and trust, between me and my burly friend, but there was, I had thought, a foundation of knowledge whereby we took each other's differences into ourselves, as well as our common histories of the cafe we had run, and, as it happened, our common serving of time in semi-monastic seminaries before we'd met – differences and similarities that had given us, I thought, ways of being in sympathy with each other while allowing for each other.

Montaigne's dearest friend, Étienne, had died, and his essay was as much about the meaning of this loss as about friendship. His big idea was loyalty, and I think I understand that, though not in the absolute way Montaigne wrote of it.

Loyalty is only real if it is constantly renewed. I worry that I have not worked enough at some friendships that have come into my life, but have let them happen more passively than the women I know who spend such time, and such complicated time, exploring and testing friendships. The sudden disappearance of my friend left me with an awareness of how patched-together, how improvised, clumsy and tentative even the most secure-seeming friendship can be.

When the philosopher and brilliant essayist Simone Weil wrote shortly before she died in 1943, 'I may lose, at any moment, through the play of circumstances over which I have no control, anything whatsoever that I possess, including things that are so intimately mine that I consider them as myself. There is nothing that I might not lose. It could happen at any moment', she seemed to be touching on the difficult truth that we run on luck and hope and chance much of the time. Why haven't I worked harder at friendships, when I know that they provide the real meaning in my life?

Some years ago, when I was told by a medical specialist that I had a 30 per cent chance of having cancer and was waiting for the results of a biopsy, I remember that, in response to these dismal odds, I had no desire to go back to work, no desire to even read — all I wanted to do was spend time with friends.

Inner worlds laid waste

To know what it is we care about – this is a gift. It should be straightforward to know this and keep it present in our lives, but it can prove to be difficult. Being the reader that I am, I have always turned to literature and fiction for answers to, or insights into, those questions that seem to need answering.

I realised some time after the ending of my friendship that I had been reading novels dealing with friendship and was not even sure how consciously I had chosen them.

For instance, I read *The Book of Strange New Things* by Michel Faber, a novel about a Christian preacher, Peter Leigh, sent to convert aliens in a galaxy ludicrously far from Earth, on a planet with an equally unlikely atmosphere benign to its human colonisers.

It is a novel about whether Leigh can be any kind of adequate friend to his wife left behind on Earth, and whether his new feelings for these aliens amounts to friendship. Though my suspension of disbelief was precarious, I found myself caring about these characters and their relationships, even the grotesquely shapeless aliens. Partly I cared about them because the book read like an essay testing ideas of friendship and loyalty that were important and urgent to the writer.

I also read at that time Haruki Murakami's novel, *Colorless Tsukuru Tazaki and His Years of Pilgrimage*, a book that came with a little game of coloured cards and stickers, and I found that I cared about Tsukuru Tazaki too, for I felt all along that Murakami's character was a thin and endearing disguise for himself (what a beautiful word that is, 'en-dearing').

The novel centred on lost friendships. I heard a tone in its voice that was the oddly flat, persistent, vulnerable and sincere searching of a man for connection with others. If Murakami's novel has a proposition it wishes to test, it would be that we only know ourselves in what images of ourselves we receive back from our friends. Without our friends we become invisible, lost.

In both those novels, the friendships are crashing to pieces in slow motion in front of the reader's helpless eyes. I wanted to shake those characters, tell them to stop and think about what they were doing, but at the same time I saw in them mirrors of myself and my experiences.

I read John Berger's *Ways of Seeing* too, on the way a human looks across an abyss of incomprehension when looking at another animal. Though language seems to connect us, it might be that language also distracts us from the actual abyss of ignorance and fear between all of us as we look, across, at each other. In his book *The Savage Mind*, Claude Lévi-Strauss quotes a study of Canadian Carrier Indians living on the Bulkley River who were able to cross that abyss between species, believing they knew what animals did and what their needs were because their men had been married to the salmon, the beaver and the bear.

I have read essays by anthropologist Robin Dunbar on the evolutionary limits to our circles of intimacy, where he suggests that most of us need three, or maybe five, truly close friends. These are the ones we lean towards with tenderness and open ourselves to with endless curiosity – those in whom we seek only the good.

My partner can name quickly four friends who qualify for her as part of this necessary circle. I find I can name two (and she is one of them), then a constellation of individual friends whose closeness to me I can't easily measure. It is this constellation that sustains me.

Recently I was away from home for three months. After two weeks away I wrote a list in the back of my diary of the friends I was missing. A little more than a dozen of these were the friends, men and women, with whom I need contact, and with whom conversations are always open-ended, surprising, intellectually stimulating, sometimes intimate, and often fun. With each of them I explore a slightly different but always essential version of myself. Graham Little wrote that 'ideal soulmates are friends who are fully aware that each has himself as his main life project'.

To live this takes some effort of imagination, and with my friend at dinner that night I might in myself have been refusing to make this effort.

There are also, it occurs to me, the friends who came as couples, with whom my partner and I share time as couples. This is itself another manifestation of friendship, one that crosses over into community, tribe and family – and no less precious than the individual intimacy of a personal friendship. For reasons I can't properly fathom, the importance of this kind of time with coupled friends has deepened as I have grown through the decades of my fifties and sixties.

Perhaps it is that the dance of conversation and ideas is so much more complex and pleasurable when there are four or more contributing. It could be too that I am absolved from the responsibility of really working at these friendships in the way one must when there are two of us. Or it might be the pang and stimulus of the knowledge that opportunities to be together are brutally diminishing as we grow older.

But to lose an individual friend from one's closest circle is to have large tracts of one's inner world laid waste for a time. My feelings over the end of this particular friendship were a kind of grief mixed with bewilderment.

It was not that the friendship was necessary to my existence but that, perhaps through habit and sympathy, it had become a fixed part of my identity. Robin Dunbar would say that by stepping away from this friendship I had made room for someone else to slip into my circle of most intimate friends, but isn't it the point of such close friends that they are in some important sense irreplaceable? This is the source of much of our distress when such friendships end.

Still learning

When I told people about what had happened in the restaurant that night, they would say, reasonably, 'Why don't you patch things up and resume your friendship?'

As I imagined how a conversation might go if I did meet my friend again, I came to understand that I had been a provocation to him. I had ceased to be the friend he needed, wanted or imagined.

What he did was dramatic. He might have called it merely dramatic. I felt it as threatening. And if we had 'patched' a friendship back together, on whose terms would this have been conducted? Would it always be that I would have to agree not to press him on questions that might lead him to throw over some table between us again?

Or worse, would I have to witness his apology, forgive him myself, and put him on his best behaviour for the rest of our friendship?

Neither of those outcomes would have patched much together. I had been hurting too over what I saw as his lack of willingness to understand, or interest in understanding, the situation from my point of view. And so it went inside me as the table and the water and the beer and the glasses came crashing down around me. I had been, in a way, married to my friend, even if he was a salmon or a bear – a creature across an abyss from me. Perhaps this was the only way out of that marriage. Perhaps he had been preparing for (moving towards?) this moment more consciously than I had been.

The ending of this friendship, it is clear, left me looking for its story. It was as if all along there must have been a narrative with a trajectory carrying us in this direction. A story is, of course, a way of testing whether an experience can take on a shape. Murakami's and Faber's novels are not themselves full-blown stories, for there is almost no plot, no shape, to their stumbling episodic structures, and, oddly enough, in both books the self-doubting lovers might or might not find that close communion with another somewhere well beyond the last page of each novel.

These novels cohere round a series of questions rather than events: what do we know and what can we know about others, what is the nature of the distance that separates one person from another, how provisional is it to know someone anyway, and what does it mean to care about someone, even someone who is a character in a novel?

When an Indian says he is married to a salmon, this can be no stranger than me saying I spent a couple of weeks on a humid planet in another galaxy with an astronaut who is a Christian preacher and an inept husband, or I spent last night in Tokyo with an engineer who builds railway stations and believes himself to be colourless, though at least two women have told him he is full of colour. But do I go to this story-making as a way of keeping my experiences less personal and more cerebral?

When I got home that night eight years ago, I sat at my kitchen table, shaking, hugging myself, talking to my grown-up children about what happened. It was the talking that helped – a narrative taking shape.

Robin Dunbar, like me, like all of us, worries at the question of what makes life so richly present to us, and why friendships seem to be at the core of this meaningfulness. He has been surveying Americans with questions about friendship for several decades, and he concludes that for many of us the small circle of intimate friendships we experience is reducing.

We are apparently lucky now, on average, if there are two people in our lives we can approach with tenderness and curiosity, with that assumption time will not matter as we talk in a low, murmuring, hive-warm way to a close friend.

My friend cannot be replaced, and it might be that we did not, in the end, imagine each other fully enough or accurately enough as we approached that last encounter. I don't know precisely what our failure was. The shock of what happened, and the shock of the friendship ending, has over the time since that dinner become a part of my history in which I remember feeling grief but am no longer caught in confused anger or guilt over it. The story of it might not have ended but it has subsided.

Perhaps in all friendships we are not only, at our best, agreeing to encountering the unique and endlessly absorbing presence of another person but, unknown to us, we're learning something about how to approach the next friendship in our lives. There is something comically inept and endearing about the possibility that one might still be learning how to be a friend right up to the end of life.

Hidden women of history: Australia's first known female voter, the famous Mrs Fanny Finch

Kacey Sinclair
PhD Candidate in History, La Trobe University

14 March 2019

On 22 January 1856, an extraordinary event in Australia's history occurred. It is not part of our collective national identity, nor has it been mythologised over the decades through song, dance or poetry. It doesn't even have a hashtag. But on this day, in the thriving gold rush town of Castlemaine, two women took to the polls and cast their votes in a democratic election.

Two days later, Melbourne newspaper *The Argus* unwittingly granted one of them posterity, writing 'two women voted – one, the famous Mrs. Fanny Finch'. Fanny Finch was a London-born businesswoman of African heritage, a single mother of four and is the first known woman to cast a vote in an Australian election.

Victorian women over the age of twenty-one (excluding Indigenous women) would not receive full unconditional suffrage until 1908. (Victorian Indigenous women were not enfranchised until 1965.) But Finch, as a local business owner who paid rates, was able to exploit a loophole in suffrage law that was yet to discriminate against gender or race.

The Municipal Institutions Act of 1854 granted suffrage to ratepaying 'persons'. The loophole was eventually closed in 1865, when 'persons' became 'men'.

Who was Fanny?

Frances Finch (nee Combe) was born in London in 1815. At eight weeks old, she was orphaned by her mother after a tryst with a footman ended in a pregnancy but no marriage proposal.

A cross-stitch sampler attributed to Frances Coombe (sic) in 1830 at the age of fifteen suggests she understood both her parents to be free people of African racial heritage (although the UK did not free slaves unconditionally until 1838). The London Foundling Hospital, where Fanny was accepted as an orphan, provided her with some protection against slavery, as well as an otherwise inaccessible education and access to an apprenticeship scheme in 'household duties'.

By 1837, a twenty-two-year-old Finch was a free, literate, educated and experienced domestic servant. In that year she was approved a labourer's free passage to the new colony of South Australia.

In Adelaide, Finch was a valued employee of Julia Wyatt, an author, artist, and wife of surgeon and the first Protector of Aborigines, Dr William Wyatt. Over the course of the next decade, Finch left their employment, married a sailor, Joseph Finch, and started a family.

By 1850, for reasons unknown, Fanny Finch had left her husband. With her four children in tow, she made her way to Victoria. She arrived in the colony twelve months before the start of the Victorian gold rush. By early 1852, she was operating a restaurant and lodging house on the Forest Creek goldfields, alongside approximately 25,000 gold-digging men and a handful of women.

There, in the fledgling township of Forest Creek, Mrs Finch's Board and Lodging House became 'the only one in which any person could get respectable accommodation'. By 1854, she had moved to nearby Castlemaine, where she ran a restaurant. She quickly became one of the town's most recognisable faces.

A successful businesswoman

Fanny Finch was a successful businesswoman, known to dress in bright blue silk, her black hair adorned with artificial flowers. Strong and robust, with an even larger personality, she was not one to shy away from attempting to remedy injustice when she saw it – be it with her words, her cooking or her fists. Evidently, she possessed visibility and power.

Her business acumen and conspicuity make it probable that her male contemporaries were unsurprised when they witnessed Finch cast her vote at the Hall of Castlemaine (now the Theatre Royal). Did the men taunt her? Encourage her? Or were they complacent? We cannot know. We do know that no one stopped her. She selected her preference and signed her name.

That afternoon, however, the two assessors of the day disallowed both Finch and the other, unknown, woman's votes. Their reasons were cited as: 'they [the women] had no right to vote'. Further details were not divulged.

Still, Walter Smith, the man for whom Fanny Finch voted, was elected to council. Smith was an agent and brewer who arrived at Forest Creek at around the same time as Finch. Little is known about what motivated her to vote for him but no one else, despite being allowed to vote for seven councillors. She was clearly determined to elect him to council.

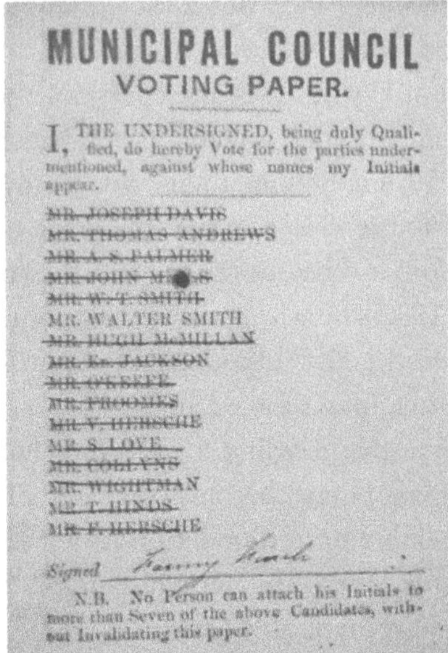

MUNICIPAL COUNCIL
VOTING PAPER.

I, THE UNDERSIGNED, being duly Qualified, do hereby Vote for the parties undermentioned, against whose names my Initials appear.

~~MR. JOSEPH DAVIS~~
~~MR. THOMAS ANDREWS~~
~~MR. A. S. PALMER~~
~~MR. JOHN M[illegible]S~~
~~MR. W. T. SMITH~~
MR. WALTER SMITH
~~MR. HUGH McMILLAN~~
~~MR. Ed. JACKSON~~
~~MR. O'KEEFE~~
~~MR. FROOMES~~
~~MR. V. HERSCHE~~
~~MR. S. LOVE~~
~~MR. COLLYNS~~
~~MR. WIGHTMAN~~
~~MR. T. HINDS~~
~~MR. F. HERSCHE~~

Signed Fanny Finch

N.B. No Person can attach his Initials to more than Seven of the above Candidates, without Invalidating this paper.

Fanny Finch's 1856 voting card. (Castlemaine Art Museum)

A rare glimpse

During colonial times, women were rarely identified by name in the press – particularly women of the working class. The 1856 *Argus* report now offers historians an unprecedented opportunity to identify an otherwise invisible minority – the 19th century Australian woman of colour – as an active participant in our political history.

Finch was a woman who, through relative privilege – wielded with her own blood, sweat and tears – refused to founder beneath the weight of a white Anglo male world of commerce. However, this came at a price. As a woman of colour occupying space in a white man's world, assaults on her success were not uncommon. Yet, she refused to disappear.

One of those assaults occurred in December 1855. Fanny Finch was fined £50 for the illicit sale of alcohol, known as 'sly-grogging'. After a month-long trial, which involved scandalous cross-examinations of miners, policemen, and even her two young sons, she was charged and fined.

Despite the exorbitant fine and the public slandering of her character and commercial integrity, Finch was not defeated. Like many businesspeople on the goldfields, she both owed money and was owed it by others, but over the following four months, she began an unprecedented campaign of self-representation.

The day following her conviction she published a letter in the local paper, accusing the local authorities of injustice (a copy of this has not survived). A month on, she cast that vote. Then a few months later, in April, she published the following advertisement.

> Mrs. Finch begs to inform the inhabitants of Castlemaine that henceforth she will carry on business for her children and would be happy to receive any outstanding debts … finding that the more she herself strives the more she is oppressed, although she can firmly state that if those who are in her debt would come forward each with one third, she will be relieved of all debt, have a good home for her family and about two thousand pounds in her pocket.
>
> Fanny Finch also begs to state that as in her affluence she was so kindly trusted, they may be sure that she, from her own free will, may some day liquidate all, but she must have her time … and in spite of what enemies she may have, she intends to keep throughout the winter ready cooked Ham, Beef Soups (a la mode) from seven in the morning to seven in the night.

The vote of the famous Fanny Finch adds a woman of colour's voice to what historian Clare Wright has described as an unorganised movement for women's rights during the 1850s.

Finch died on 15 October 1863, aged forty-eight. She was remembered as 'a strong minded woman' with 'a genuine tenderness of heart, ever ready to serve another in distress … without the slightest ostentation'.

She was given a public burial in an unmarked grave at Castlemaine Cemetery.

Editor's note: Following publication of this essay, the names of three other women who voted in an election before Fanny Finch have become known to the author. They are Ellen Fraser, Margaret Cox and Ellen Murnan. Their names were recorded in the election report of the Warrnambool Council election. These women voted the week prior to Fanny Finch and their votes were allowed.

From delicate teens to fierce women, Simone Biles's athleticism and advocacy have changed gymnastics forever

Ella Donald
Casual Academic, University of Queensland

4 October 2019

At the 1976 Olympics in Montreal, gymnastics got what it was looking for: an image.

Romania's Nadia Comăneci was a tiny fourteen-year-old, leaping on the floor with a pixie-like grace, moving between the bars with lightning-fast precision. On her first bar routine, she received a perfect ten: the first ever ten in Olympic gymnastics.

She would go on to receive seven perfect tens over the course of the 1976 games.

Comăneci became an icon of the sport, and the image of a young, lithe girl has endured.

Even through the loss of the perfect ten and the introduction of open scoring – favouring strength and power – women's gymnastics is still too often dismissed as a sport of frivolity, dominated by children, meek and prepubescent, discouraged from expressing themselves.

Simone Biles – a confident, powerful woman at the peak of her powers in her early twenties – is a change to gymnastics that was inevitable but is simultaneously one she has come to symbolise.

She is both the greatest gymnast ever and unlike any gymnast the world ever has seen.

A punishing gymnastics monarch

Comăneci had her run in 1976 thanks to husband-and-wife coaching team Béla and Márta Károlyi. To understand the pair is to understand the image of the Olympic champion.

Béla was a former boxing champion and member of the national hammer throwing team, later studying gymnastics while at the Romania College of Physical Education.

In his final year at the college, he coached the women's team, which included Márta. After starting their own class in the town where Béla grew up, they were invited to create a national school for gymnastics.

It was when he was training young girls, handpicked for the sport based on their specific body types, he first encountered six-year-old Comăneci.

The Károlyis produced outstanding athletes who seemingly achieved the impossible with focus and ease. In 1981, the pair defected to the United States, and continued their reign in a new country, building a gym in rural Texas they named Károlyi Ranch. By 1984, Béla had coached new Olympic champions in Mary Lou Retton and Julianne McNamara.

In 1999, Béla was appointed the national team coordinator; and the isolated Károlyi Ranch was designated the US women's national training centre. For many years, this gym was a mythologised site of gymnast creation: it would later extensively figure in the sexual abuse trial of former national team doctor Larry Nassar.

The Károlyis had exacting – and often damaging – standards. Gymnasts felt compelled to train and compete with broken bones and other injuries. They divested the diverse body shapes that once filled the sport for a perpetual state of prepubescence, maintained by punishing overtraining and disordered eating: 1996 Olympic champion Dominique Moceanu has said the athletes were restricted to 900 calories per day.

Numerous former athletes – including Romanian team members Rodica Dunca, Emilia Eberle and Ecaterina Szabo – claim they were subject to regular beatings for making mistakes; and Joan Ryan's headline-making 1995 book *Little Girls in Pretty Boxes* contained various allegations of verbal and psychological abuse.

As hundreds of women would later say in victim impact statements against Nassar, this environment would not only create the 'ideal' gymnastic body but would also create demure girls taught to never talk back.

In 2008, Moceanu spoke about the abuse she had faced as a young gymnast – in 2018 she told *Deadspin*, the sport blog, this decision to speak out had ruined her career.

Some of the Károlyis' athletes have only praised them; others, like Betty Okino in *Little Girls in Pretty Boxes*, have argued the medals justified the means.

Under the Károlyis' reign from the 1980s until Márta's retirement in 2016, the US women's gymnastics team seemed to have superpowers.

Competing until they break

Gymnastics is a sport requiring strength and endurance to withstand the G-forces of landings on the floor, a narrow bar or thin mat. But it had come to favour bodies possessing neither. As a result, young girls were pushed to breaking point – with athletes disappearing from the sport in their mid-teens.

Within three years of commencing her senior career, Retton won two American Cups, two American Classics, and the all-round competition at the Olympics, and retired.

Within two years, Okino had won two National Championship medals, three medals at World Championships, contributed to the first American Olympic team victory in 1992, and retired.

In 2016, Laurie Hernandez made her senior debut, winning the City of Jesolo Trophy in Italy, gold for the team at the Pacific Rim Gymnastics Championships, four medals at the US Nationals, and a gold and a silver at the Olympics. She hasn't competed since.

Countless others followed the same trajectory.

It remains a sport of youth. Olympic gold medallist Jordyn Wieber joined the elite level of the sport at eleven, and at thirteen she became the second youngest American Cup champion ever; her fellow 2012 gold Olympian Kyla Ross was twelve when she beat more seasoned future teammates Aly Raisman and McKayla Maroney at the US Classic.

Biles bucked the trend from the beginning. When she was thirteen, she placed forty-forth in the pre-elite national championships.

In 2013, when they were both fifteen, Katelyn Ohashi won gold at the American Cup and Biles won silver. It would be Ohashi's last elite competition.

It was also the last time anyone would ever beat Biles at the all-around event.

At nineteen years old at the 2016 Rio Olympics, she was already considered old for the sport. She collected five medals – four of them gold.

It was the performance of a lifetime.

A new mould of gymnast

Watching Biles is the opposite to watching Comăneci.

Like the Romanian, she stands under 5 feet at 142 centimetres – diminutive when compared with many other athletes.

However, Biles has something the 1976 champion did not – explosive strength. She is, as *Deadspin* describes her, a 'power gymnast' who 'racked up difficulty on beam using tumbling skills instead of dance elements'.

Comăneci was a consummate performer, but frequently displayed a sense of apprehension, as though liable to snap from a bad landing: a body not built to withstand the force demanded of it.

But Biles competes with the muscle mass and power of male athletes, performing with toned quads, pectorals and triceps. Her skills defy gravity, going beyond what was thought to be possible in the sport. Frequently possessing so much energy she bounces out of bounds even after a long pass, she gives a feeling of boundless possibility.

In gymnastics, a new skill is named after the first athlete to perform it at an international competition. 'The Biles' on floor is two flips and half a twist, in a laid-out position, backwards.

At the 2019 World Championships, we will likely have the Biles II: three twists and two flips. Watching footage of this pre-championships, you get the sense she needs to add *at least* another twist.

But she is not only a revelation in terms of her skills. Her candour – playfulness, jazzy artistry and irresistible entertainment value – is refreshing, a departure from the straitlaced discipline viewers had become accustomed to, and freely incorporates Latin-inspired beats and choreography.

The racism Biles has faced is often disguised as critiques not of her but of her athleticism and performance. In 2013 David Ciaralli, the Italian Gymnastics Federation's spokesperson, wrote on Facebook: 'the Code of Points is opening chances for coloured people (known to be more powerful) and penalising the typical Eastern European elegance, which, when gymnastics was more artistic and less acrobatic, allowed Russia and Romania to dominate the field.'

As recently as this past August, former US national coordinator Valeri Liukin said: 'In the Code of Points, difficulty is very valued now. Of course, this suits African Americans. They're very explosive – look at the NBA, who's playing and jumping there?'

Showing the difficulty

The child prodigies of the sport once telegraphed an air of effortlessness: a confidence and ease that presented tumbling across an inches-wide bar as little more than frivolity in the playground.

But as Biles constantly pushes higher levels of difficulty, she also performs with the gravitas of effort. Despite her ability to turn an exhausting tumbling pass and still be left with energy to burn, she exudes difficulty.

After close to a decade in the training cycle of elite gymnastics – a lengthy tenure in a world of quick rises and falls – her body is likely growing tired from repetitive pounding, regardless of deft pacing.

But there's another difference, which has become more pronounced with the passing of time: Biles's personality. Just as the sport was previously a place for girls' bodies, the athletes were expected to be softly spoken, with childlike politeness. But Biles is brave and outspoken.

When Mary Bono was appointed CEO of USA gymnastics in 2018, she lasted three days after Biles publicly called her out for racism against Black athletes. Bono had tweeted about Nike's partnership with activist and NFL quarterback Colin Kaepernick, who kneeled as a sign of protest during a pre-game national anthem in 2016:

> Playing in a charity golf tournament raising money for our nation's Special Forces operators and their families. Unfortunately had these shoes in my bag. Luckily I had a marker in my bag too...

Bono's tweet was accompanied by a photo of her colouring in the Nike 'swoosh' on a pair of shoes with a black pen, mirroring others that oppose Nike's work with Kaepernick. The tweet was deleted shortly after being posted, but before it was, Biles responded: '*mouth drop* don't worry, it's not like we needed a smarter usa gymnastics president or any sponsors or anything.'

In the wake of the Larry Nassar sexual abuse scandal embroiling peak body USA Gymnastics, Biles has been a rare and consistent voice from a current elite athlete – vocal at competitions and on social media, as more failings of accountability and to protect athlete welfare emerge, wisened and hardened with each new revelation.

'You had one job,' she said in August.

'You literally had one job and you couldn't protect us, and it is just really sad because now every time I go to the doctor or training, I get worked on. I don't want to get worked on, but my body hurts, I'm 22 and at the end of the day that's my fifth rotation and I have to go to therapy.'

In January 2018, as Nassar was being sentenced, Biles tweeted a statement about the trauma she associated with the Károlyi Ranch: 'It breaks my heart even more to think that, as I work towards my dream of competing in Tokyo 2020, I will have to continually return to the same training facility where I was abused.'

This would not eventuate. Thanks to Biles's criticism, USA Gymnastics ended its nearly four-decade relationship with the Károlyi Ranch.

The end of an era

Biles declared the 2020 Olympics [would] be her last meet.

'I feel like my body's gone through a lot and it's kind of just falling apart – not that you can actually tell but I really feel it a lot of the time,' she said in London.

If measuring her career only with the hardware she has collected, it would be remarkable – even now, as she goes into the preliminary rounds of the 2019 World Championships in Stuttgart, Germany, she has the most all-around titles in the history of the competition – and is the most decorated American gymnast of all time.

But the way Biles has shaped the sport with her displays of strength – as an athlete and as an advocate – will arguably be the biggest mark she leaves on it.

Biles is a far cry from Comăneci and the diminutive gymnasts of the 1970s. But the world of gymnastics is also changing around her.

Internationally, she's far from the oldest current competitor – in recent years, smaller programs have nurtured more and more experienced athletes through their twenties, thirties and beyond in the name of retaining top talent.

Among others, at the 2019 Championships Biles will compete against the Netherlands' Sanne Wevers (aged twenty-eight), Germany's Kim Bui (thirty), Brazil's Jade Barbosa (twenty-eight), and long-time fan favourite Aliya Mustafina (twenty-five) from Russia, who declared 'it was easier to give birth than to restore inbars' when recommencing training as a new mother in 2017.

Also competing will be Oksana Chusovitina – forty-four years old, in her seventeenth World Championships, and still one of the best vaulters in the world.

Biles heads into the 2019 World Artistic Gymnastics Championships as the firm favourite. She is twenty-two, and at the peak of her powers. By this time next year, we will have seen her perform for the final time, undoubtedly having added a new clutch of medals to her collection and leaving more eponymous skills behind.

It's difficult to predict who will follow in her footsteps, but she'll leave a legacy to be felt for years to come: a trend of women staying in the sport longer, training smarter, and owning their strength as athletes, and as women.

Diversity in race and physique among elite gymnastics is becoming increasingly common. It's a far cry from decades ago – the US didn't have Luci Collins, its first African-American Olympic gymnast, until 1980.

For the spectators, the sport is perhaps now less about the artistry of gymnastics, and more about gymnastics as a sport of agility and strength.

Today, forty-three years after Comăneci became the face of gymnastics, the sport has a new image.

Editor's note: Biles said in April 2021 that this year's delayed Olympics will be her final as an all-round gymnast, but she has said she may return in 2024 as a specialist on some events.

PART III

Events that changed the world

The backlash against Black Lives Matter is just more evidence of injustice

David Smith
Senior Lecturer in American Politics and Foreign Policy, Academic Director of the US Studies Centre, University of Sydney

1 November 2017

In white-dominated societies, nearly any demand for equality by people of colour is met by a backlash couched in terms of white victimhood. This has been as true for Black Lives Matter as it was for the civil rights movement.

Just as Black Lives Matter went global, so did the backlash.

One popular (and self-serving) theory holds that white identity politics is merely a response to movements like Black Lives Matter. But this gets the story backwards. Black Lives Matter is a response to white supremacy. The anger harnessed by figures like Donald Trump and Rudy Giuliani is the anger of white privilege forced to defend itself.

'All Lives Matter' and 'Blue Lives Matter' are two of the most prominent rhetorical manifestations of the backlash. Both played major roles in the media coverage of and political response to Black Lives Matter.

All Lives Matter

The hashtag and slogan 'All Lives Matter' is a declaration of 'colourblindness', which legal academic Ian Haney-López describes as 'the dominant etiquette around race' today. As is so often the case when it comes to race, liberal rhetoric serves conservative ends.

'All Lives Matter' erases a long past and present of systemic inequality in the US. It represents a refusal to acknowledge that the state does not value all lives in the same way. It reduces the problem of racism to individual prejudice and casts African-Americans as aggressors against a colourblind post-civil rights order in which white people no longer 'see race'.

This kind of rhetoric is hardly new, as we learn from sociologist Eduardo Bonilla-Silva's book *Racism Without Racists: Color-Blind Racism and the Persistence of Racial Inequality in America*. It is the most up-to-date articulation of how most white people view racism (as a rare, archaic and unfortunate psychological disposition) as opposed to how most people of colour see it (as institutionalised and systemic).

Under the white understanding, talking about systemic racism is itself racist, because it conjures into existence 'racial divides' that are invisible to whites who believe themselves to be free of prejudice.

There is no better example of this than Giuliani, the former New York Mayor, who is a famous proponent of 'stop and frisk' policing and a long-time master of backlash politics. He told CNN Black Lives Matter is 'inherently racist' because 'it divides us ... All lives matter: white lives, Black lives, all lives.'

Giuliani went on to say: 'Black Lives Matter never protests when every 14 hours someone is killed in Chicago, probably 70–80% of the time by a Black person. Where are they then? Where are they when a young Black child is killed?'

This argument is a popular one in backlash politics. It holds that Black Lives Matter only cares about Black life when white people are responsible for taking it, thus ignoring and displacing Black responsibility for violence in Black communities.

In November 2015, Donald Trump tweeted an infographic purporting to show Black people were responsible for 97 per cent of murders of Black people and 82 per cent of murders of white people. Both 'statistics' are wrong, the latter monstrously so: African-Americans accounted for about 15 per cent of murders of whites, according to FBI data. (See '2014 Crime in the United States'.)

This twisted tribal accounting deliberately obscures Black Lives Matter's critique of violence, inequality and failings at all levels of the criminal justice system. Like the slogan 'All Lives Matter', it is a way of changing the subject.

It also exposes the myths of colourblind rhetoric. Many white people are more than happy to 'see colour' when assigning blame for Black deaths, and to treat that as the end of the issue.

'All Lives Matter' has not always served as the powerful rebuke of Black Lives Matter that the backlash intends. One strategy by online activists has been to refuse to acknowledge the disingenuous binary of 'Black' and 'all'.

Academic Nikita Carney notes in her study of the #BlackLivesMatter and #AllLivesMatter hashtags ('All lives matter, but so does race: Black Lives Matter and the evolving role of social media') that some Black Twitter users simply used both when calling for protests against police violence, effectively disarming the dishonest critique implied by All Lives Matter.

Alicia Garza, one of the creators of the #BlackLivesMatter hashtag, explained in 2014 how Black lives mattering is a precondition for all lives mattering:

> Black Lives Matter doesn't mean your life isn't important – it means that Black lives, which are seen as without value within white supremacy, are important to your liberation. Given the disproportionate impact state violence has on Black lives, we understand that when Black people in this country get free, the benefits will be wide-reaching and transformative for society as a whole.
>
> When we are able to end the hyper-criminalisation and sexualisation of Black people and end the poverty, control and surveillance of Black people, every single person in this world has a better shot at getting and staying free. When Black people get free, everybody gets free.

Blue Lives Matter

While campaigning for the presidency in late 2015, Trump said that if elected he would use an executive order to make the death penalty mandatory for anyone who killed a police officer. The US President has no such authority, but Trump was attuned to the politics of the backlash.

The idea of a Black Lives Matter-inspired 'war on cops' plays a powerful role in the backlash imagination. In 2014 and 2016, there were three ambush murders of multiple officers in New York, Baton Rouge and Dallas. Each was committed by a different lone gunman who sought revenge against police for their violence against Black communities.

These atrocities received blanket media coverage and became a major theme of the 2016 Republican National Convention. Milwaukee Sheriff David Clarke opened his speech by declaring 'blue lives matter', blaming Black Lives Matter for 'the collapse of social order'.

Giuliani, speaking shortly afterwards, claimed most Americans do not feel safe and 'they fear for our police officers who are being targeted'.

In Australia, *The Daily Telegraph's* Miranda Devine blamed Black Lives Matter for the killing of an unarmed Australian woman in Minnesota by a police officer in July this year.

Devine claimed police were 'more prone to make tragic mistakes' because they felt under siege following a 'wave of ambushes and assassinations' incited by Black Lives Matter. She also asserted, baselessly, that 'their entire movement is built on a lie' and that 'Black Americans are more likely to kill cops than be killed by cops'.

In fact, it is estimated police killed more than four times as many Black Americans last year as the other way round. There is no evidence of a resurgent 'war on police'.

In 2016, sixty-four officers were shot dead, a much-remarked jump from forty-one in 2015. But this remains within the average range of police deaths for the past ten years, which itself represents a steep drop from previous decades. An average of 115 were murdered each year in the 1970s, when the population was two-thirds what it is now. So far in 2017, thirty-six officers have been shot dead.

It is far harder to say whether killings by police are rising or falling, because no reliable data have been kept until recently. Thousands of law enforcement agencies participate in the FBI's annual Uniform Crime Report, but according to PolitiFact 'just a small fraction of them willingly provide data on deadly force and justifiable homicides within their departments'.

This has led to recent data collection efforts by NGOs and media outlets, but without trustworthy numbers from previous years to allow for historical comparison. 'The Counted', a project by *The Guardian*, found police killed 1093 people in 2016, 266 of them African-American.

Nonetheless, the Blue Lives Matter backlash has borne fruit. According to a *Huffington Post* report, thirty-three 'Blue Lives Matter' bills have been introduced in fourteen states in 2017, following fifteen such bills in 2016. The purpose of these bills is to extend hate crime protections to members of law enforcement, thus increasing penalties for crimes committed against them.

Most of these bills have failed, but they have become law in Louisiana and Kentucky. A similar bill went into the committee stage in South Carolina, which doesn't have a hate crimes statute and automatically puts the death penalty on the table for the murder of police officers.

Such laws are profoundly unnecessary, which is why most such bills don't become laws. Penalties in all fifty states are already more severe for crimes committed against law enforcement officers.

However, Blue Lives Matter bills serve a political purpose. They suggest members of racial minorities are somehow more 'protected' than police officers, who are the real victims.

When Louisiana's law was signed, a Blue Lives Matter national spokesman said it was 'important symbolically because it advises there is a value to the lives of police officers'.

Bestowing the status of a victim class on police is a grotesque distortion of reality and a symptom of structural violence. Police do a dangerous job, but there has never been any question that their lives matter. Criminal justice is never pursued more vigorously than when a police officer is killed.

Slain police officers deserve to be mourned. But those slain by police officers deserve at least to be counted. Black Lives Matter draws attention not just to police violence but to the many deep imbalances in how the state values human life.

#MeToo is not enough. It has yet to shift the power imbalances that would bring about gender equality

Eva Cox
Professorial Fellow, Jumbunna IHL, University of Technology Sydney

19 March 2018

When news of the allegations against Hollywood producer Harvey Weinstein broke last October, it unleashed a torrent of emotion, especially on social media, offering permission to disclose current and past experiences of sexual harassment and assault. In an unprecedented quantum of use, it offered many angry and upset women accessible ways of venting often long-repressed feelings. It also gave rise to the #MeToo movement.

The volume and breadth of the responses raise many serious questions about the presumed 'equality' gains of women. Over the past seventy years, after Simone de Beauvoir, Betty Friedan and Germaine Greer started debates that drove the second-wave feminist movement, we have achieved serious changes to our legal status, paid employment, and roles in public life.

However, the torrents of anger and complaints from #MeToo raise issues of whether gender powers have really been redefined, both locally and in most Western countries. Have we really made the essential cultural shifts that ensure women are no longer the 'second sex', living in worlds devised, defined and controlled by men?

The intentions of the second wave covered more than making women equal to men (in their terms, as were then defined). We intended to create the changes that allowed women and men to redefine what matters, to ensure we were no longer seen as primarily sexual or reproductive objects.

The current debate is just further evidence we failed to make the necessary power shifts. And macho male resistance to women's power may also be increasing.

The increasing reports and complaints we see in the media and the fact that, on average, one woman a week is murdered by her current or former partner, according to data from the Australian Institute of Health and Welfare, suggest current gender power imbalances are creating far too many damaging and unequal male–female relationships. Too many men, including those in power, express their ego, insecurities, problems and frustrations by dominating, bullying, controlling, undermining and embarrassing women.

The public appetite for equitable social changes seems to be receding, replaced with deteriorating social and political trust alongside growing nostalgia and tribalism. So, there appears to be little hope for more progressive power shifts to create more gender fairness.

There has been some optimism that the volume of protests and outpourings would generate public movements for change. But, like most forms of protest, they offer evidence of problems but fail to tackle the broader causes and how to fix them.

Part of the ongoing problem is the lack of serious cultural change programs that shift structures. The emphasis is still on using the law to handle individual complaints via either conciliation or charges.

Conciliation, when it works, does not allocate blame and is usually confidential, so is not a change agent. If charges are laid, the process often damages the complainant, as they are questioned and frequently shamed, even if they win. Many lose, and the process really becomes a social change deterrent.

There are multiple recorded problems with the individualised complaints model, as those accused seek to crush or shame accusers. A prime recent example of this is the allegations of sexual harassment against former Deputy Prime Minister Barnaby Joyce. When this accusation came to light, the personal details of the female complainant were published, and her desire for confidentiality was ignored.

There are many other stories of how those who seek individual complaints are punished: lost jobs, character assassination, being labelled as 'difficult', and so on.

While many of the reports are of serious crimes that need to be reported to police, others are of behaviour that ranges from offensive and annoying to bad, crass and stupid. What they share are macho power assumptions and powerless feminised responses, all of which ensures they are inadequately tackled.

Accusations of crimes create often expensive court cases that cause damage to a complainant even if she wins. Thus, formal justice may offer little relief.

Yes, the system does punish those convicted as perpetrators, but it deters few, as individualised measures do not affect most of the wider societal groups that misuse their macho power.

Legal processes, even if based on rights, do not really effect the serious social change to attitudes or power that real gender equity will require. We need to address the social mores and related power structures that reinforce male power and support toxic masculinity.

How can we use the current explosion of evidence and outrage to trigger the needed changes?

We are still in the early days of the 'new' media as social change agents. Some positives: celebratory protests at award ceremonies and the wearing of supportive signs and colours have increased media coverage and the visibility of public support. There are discussions of increased resources for legal actions against perpetrators, and for more funding support to care for victims.

But these 'solutions' are similar to those being pursued in the many campaigns against domestic violence, helping survivors. While these responses are needed in the short term, we must realise they will not drive the cultural and gendered power changes we need. If 'clicktivism' replaces wider political action and campaigns for change, we go backwards.

If we are serious about the abuse of gender-based power, we must look at its causes and make structural and cultural changes. We must overcome the serious, widespread gender-biased socialisation of boys and girls, in most cases long before they reach puberty.

Basic assumptions about gender roles still create beliefs about being an acceptable boy (stand up for yourself) or girl (be nice and read people's feelings). These offer sure-fire paths to toxic masculinity and passive femininity.

These emerged in a recent BBC documentary, *No More Boys and Girls: Can Our Kids Go Gender Free?*, broadcast on the ABC. It showed seven-year-olds displaying very stereotypical views of preferring male over female when it came to confidence in skills and leadership. It also showed how removing school and home items that reinforced gender roles could reduce the different socialisations – in other words, it's not genetic.

Given all of that, my concern is that #MeToo and related expressions of anger are failing to fix causes that increase macho-driven gender power imbalances. This means we need real, practical solutions to bridge the gender divide and stop supporting toxic masculinity.

Coronavirus: Ten reasons why you ought not to panic

Ignacio López-Goñi
Professor of Microbiology, Universidad de Navarra

7 March 2020

Regardless of whether we classify the new coronavirus as a pandemic, it is a serious issue. In less than two months, it has spread over several continents. 'Pandemic' means sustained and continuous transmission of the disease, simultaneously in more than three different geographical regions. 'Pandemic' does not refer to the lethality of a virus but to its transmissibility and geographical extension.

What we certainly have is a pandemic of fear. The entire planet's media is gripped by coronavirus. It is right that there is deep concern and mass planning for worst-case scenarios. And, of course, the repercussions move from the global health sphere into business and politics.

But it is also right that we must not panic. It would be wrong to say there is good news coming out of COVID-19, but there are causes for optimism; reasons to think there may be ways to contain and defeat the virus. And lessons to learn for the future.

1. We know what it is

The first cases of AIDS were described in June 1981 and it took more than two years to identify the virus (HIV) causing the disease. With COVID-19, the first cases of severe pneumonia were reported in China on 31 December 2019 and by 7 January the virus had already been identified. The genome was available on day ten.

We already know it is a new coronavirus from group 2B, of the same family as SARS, which we have called SARSCoV2. The disease is called COVID-19. It is thought to be related to coronavirus from bats. Genetic analyses have confirmed it has a recent natural origin (between the end of November and the beginning of December) and that, although viruses live by mutating, its mutation rate may not be very high.

2. We know how to detect the virus

Since 13 January, a test to detect the virus has been available.

3. The situation is improving in China

The strong control and isolation measures imposed by China are paying off. For several weeks now, the number of cases diagnosed every day is decreasing. A very detailed epidemiological follow-up is being carried out in other countries; outbreaks are very specific to areas, which can allow them to be controlled more easily.

4. Eighty per cent of cases are mild

The disease causes no symptoms or is mild in 81 per cent of cases. Of course, in 14 per cent it can cause severe pneumonia and in 5 per cent it can become critical or even fatal. It is still unclear what the death rate may be. But it could be lower than some estimates so far

5. People recover

Much of the reported data relates to the increase in the number of confirmed cases and the number of deaths, but most infected people are cured. There are thirteen times more cured cases than deaths, and that proportion is increasing.

6. Symptoms appear mild in children

Only 3 per cent of cases occur in people under twenty, and mortality in people under forty is only 0.2 per cent. Symptoms are so mild in children it can go unnoticed.

7. The virus can be wiped clean

The virus can be effectively inactivated from surfaces with a solution of ethanol (62–71 per cent alcohol), hydrogen peroxide (0.5 per cent hydrogen peroxide) or sodium hypochlorite (0.1 per cent bleach), in just one minute. Frequent handwashing with soap and water is the most effective way to avoid contagion.

8. Science is on it, globally

It is the age of international science cooperation. After just over a month, 164 articles could be accessed in PubMed on COVID-19 or SARS-COV-2, as well as many others available in repositories of articles not yet reviewed. They are preliminary works on vaccines, treatments, epidemiology, genetics and phylogeny, diagnosis, clinical aspects, etc.

These articles were written by some 700 authors, distributed throughout the planet. It is cooperative science, shared and open. In 2003, with the SARS epidemic, it took more than a year to reach less than half that number of articles. In addition, most scientific journals have left their publications as open access on the subject of coronaviruses.

9. There are already vaccine prototypes

Our ability to design new vaccines is spectacular. There are already more than eight projects underway seeking a vaccine against the new coronavirus. There are groups that work on vaccination projects against similar viruses.

The vaccine group of the University of Queensland, in Australia, has announced it is already working on a prototype using the technique called 'molecular clamp', a novel technology. This is just one example that could allow vaccine production in record time. Prototypes may soon be tested on humans.

10. Antiviral trials are underway

Vaccines are preventive. Right now, the treatment of people who are already sick is important. There are already more than eighty clinical trials analysing coronavirus treatments. These are antivirals that have been used for other infections, which are already approved and that we know are safe.

One of those that has already been tested in humans is remdesivir, a broad-spectrum antiviral still under study, which has been tested against Ebola and SARS/MERS.

Another candidate is chloroquine, an antimalarial that has also been seen to have potent antiviral activity. It is known that chloroquine blocks viral infection by increasing the pH of the endosome, which is needed for the fusion of the virus with the cell, thus inhibiting its entry. It has been demonstrated that this compound blocks the new coronavirus in vitro and it is already being used in patients with coronavirus pneumonia.

Other proposed trials are based on the use of oseltamivir (which is used against the influenza virus), interferon beta-1b (protein with antiviral function), antisera from people who recovered or monoclonal antibodies to neutralise the virus. New therapies have been proposed with inhibitory substances, such as baricitinib selected by artificial intelligence.

The 1918 flu pandemic caused more than 25 million deaths in less than twenty-five weeks. Could something similar happen now? Probably not; we have never been better prepared to fight a pandemic.

Editor's note: This article was published in March 2020, approximately two months after the first case outside China. Subsequent studies have found hydroxychloroquine, lopinavir and ritonavir to be ineffective; however, studies for other antivirals are still ongoing.

Despite 432 Indigenous deaths in custody since 1991, no one has ever been convicted. Racist silence and complicity are to blame

---

Alison Whittaker
Research Fellow, University of Technology Sydney

3 June 2020

You probably know the details of the death of George Floyd. He was a doting father and musician. He was killed when a police officer,

Derek Chauvin, knelt on his neck for nearly nine minutes while he cried out, 'I can't breathe!' Chauvin was charged with third-degree murder; three other officers were also charged over their involvement.

Do you know about David Dungay Jr? He was a Dunghutti man, an uncle. He had a talent for poetry that made his family endlessly proud. He was held down by six corrections officers in a prone position until he died, after twice being injected with sedatives, because he ate rice crackers in his cell.

Dungay's last words were also, 'I can't breathe.'

An officer replied, 'If you can talk, you can breathe.'

At the end of a long inquest that stretched to almost four years, the coroner declined to refer the officers involved in Dungay's death to prosecutors (who might have considered charges) or to disciplinary bodies.

Paul Silva, Dungay's nephew and among the most powerful advocates for justice, said as he was leaving court, 'What am I meant to do now? Go home, look at the ground? Tell my uncle, "Sorry, Unc, there's no justice here!"'

In June 2020, he told *The Guardian*:

> When I heard [George Floyd] say 'I can't breathe' for the first time I had to stop... My solidarity is with them because I do know the pain they are feeling. And as for the Aboriginal deaths in our backyard... it's not in the public as much as it should be.

A perception that Indigenous deaths in custody are expected

Many people in Australia know more about police and prison violence in the US, another settler colony, than the same violence that happens here. Both are deserving of our attention and action, so what's behind the curious silence on First Nations deaths in custody in Australia?

Aboriginal and Torres Strait Islander peoples raised this concern long before 2020 in the media and social media. Why do we have to? The reasons are complex, but they boil down to a system of complicity and perceived normality in Indigenous deaths at the hands of police and prison officers. The settler Australian public simply does not see Indigenous deaths in custody as an act of violence, but rather as a comorbidity.

Amanda Porter, an Indigenous scholar of policing and criminal justice, researches media coverage of Indigenous deaths in custody in Australia compared with the US. She notes differences in the way the media covered the 2014 police shooting of eighteen-year-old Michael Brown in Ferguson, Missouri, compared with the 2004 killing of Mulrunji Doomadgee while in custody on Palm Island. Both were Black men killed by police while being spuriously detained, with neither death resulting in a conviction.

> The choice of language is important: it evokes a certain response in the reader and shapes our understandings of events. In the case of Palm Island, the often-repeated meta-narrative of so-called 'dysfunctional' and 'lawless' Aboriginal communities served to justify further acts of colonial violence.

Why the silence?

Since 1991, some 432 Indigenous people (possibly more) have died in custody. In my 2018 pilot study on a sample of 134 Indigenous deaths in custody since the Royal Commission into Aboriginal Deaths in Custody, I found coroners considered referring just eleven deaths to prosecutors and only ended up referring five. Of those, only two made it to court, and both resulted in quashed indictments or acquittals.

These are monumental figures. They are also stories of deep systemic complicity, both before and after death. And they are full lives, with loved ones who mourn and fight for them. Aunty Tanya Day, for instance, campaigned for justice for her uncle who died in custody, and later died in custody herself. In late August 2020, news broke that the police officers involved in the Yorta Yorta woman's death would not face any criminal charges.

The scale of devastation is unthinkable – and violent, and racist.

What makes Australian silence about deaths in custody so especially bizarre is that, unlike the US, we have a mandatory legal review of every death in custody or police presence. Each case, regardless of its circumstances, goes before a coroner who investigates the cause of death.

Just as public political will is always changing, so is law and legal strategy. Compared with the campaigns for justice for Black people killed by police in the US, which have made relative gains, families in Australia are faced with vastly different processes. For many families here, footage is not available until years after the death of their loved one. Revealing footage of a loved one who has died is a complex cultural and spiritual space to navigate, with protocols in some nations and clans governing how and if those who have passed away can be spoken about or represented. At the same time, criticism is bubbling that Black families across the world are faced with these grievous decisions, sharing the last traumas and indignities of their loved ones in order to mobilise the public or draw attention to state violence.

Coroners have offered mixed responses, and each state's and territory's coroner approaches the question in a slightly different way.

After the death of Ms Dhu, a Yamatji woman, in police custody in Western Australia in 2014, persistent advocacy from her family and media organisations prompted the coroner to release footage of her treatment before her death. Coroner Ros Fogliani did so 'in order to assist with the fair and accurate reporting of my findings on inquest'.

However, in 2019, NSW deputy coroner Derek Lee initially declined to release footage showing the circumstances of Dungay's death, citing cultural respect, sensitivity for his family and secrecy over prison procedures. Members of Dungay's family, who had applied to have the vision released, responded with exasperation. It was eventually shown on the opening day of the inquest, although the fuller footage requested by the family remains suppressed from public view.

Other ways in which families are silenced

There are other transparency issues that give a legal structure to silence about Indigenous deaths in custody.

For one thing, there appears to be a new push in non-publication or suppression orders being sought by state parties in coroners' courts. In Dungay's inquest, for instance, the media was ordered not to publish the names, addresses or any other identifying features (including photographs) of twenty-one NSW Corrective Services staff members. There have been other suppression orders in deaths in custody matters before criminal courts, such as the identity of the officer facing a murder charge in the death of Yamatji woman Joyce Clarke in Western Australia in 2019.

Officers in South Australia are also going to some effort to avoid testifying before the inquest into the death of Wayne Fella Morrison, a Wiradjuri, Kookatha and Wirangu man, or even speak with investigators, on the grounds of penalty privilege. This is essentially a protection from being compelled to provide evidence that could expose that person to a civil or professional penalty. So far, they have not been successful in claiming the privilege, despite taking the matter to the SA Supreme Court.

Latoya Rule, Morrison's sibling, has written that

> investigations surrounding the cause of death in prisons can have a great impact for our grieving families to at least get an account of what happened to our loved ones in the absence of our care. It can also raise the spotlight on the behaviours of correctional and police officers – like those that piled atop of my brother's body.

Outside of coroners' courts, for all matters there is the threat of sub judice contempt, when media coverage may pose a prejudicial threat to a potential trial. This carries a risk for families who speak out about their loved ones' deaths in a way that even implies something happened or someone did something. Sub judice contempt poses liability to them personally when they speak out, but it could also jeopardise their push for justice.

This puts First Nations peoples at the mercy of what can be raised before a jury, judge or coroner. With lengthy procedural delays, this can also mean a case is hard to talk about publicly for years.

This is problematic given that timely publicity about deaths in custody is what drives attention. Taleah Reynolds, the sister of Nathan Reynolds, who died in custody in New South Wales in 2018, said, 'We're coming up to a year since he died and we still don't know anything more. I feel like they don't have any remorse; they hide behind the system. No one's held accountable, that's the most frustrating part.'

Combined with plaintiff-friendly defamation laws, media ignorance and racist editorial decisions, and a lack of institutional support for Indigenous journalism, this contributes to some of the hedging language we see around police brutality in Australia, like someone 'appearing' to do something captured on video.

All of this leaves our public discourse full of Blak bodies but curiously empty of the people who put them there.

The power of public campaigning

Prosecution or referral seems to come only from cases where First Nations families have strong public advocacy and community groundswells behind them, and strategic litigation resources (not just inquest legal aid).

As the late Wangerriburra and Birri Gubba leader Sam Watson said of the campaign for justice for the death of Mulrunji Doomadgee on Palm Island:

> Unfortunately, the government had to be dragged to this point screaming and kicking every inch of the way. Every time there's been a breakdown in the procedure, the family and community on Palm Island are being subjected to more trauma, drama and unnecessary grandstanding by politicians.

In July 2020, three deaths were either before prosecutors or in their early stages of prosecution. All have been part of growing, public campaigns driven by the families and communities – although many others, like Dungay's family, have done the same and still been faced with institutional complicity.

Clearly, there is much legal structure that supports this silence, but the basis of the silence itself is colonisation and white supremacy. As journalist and Darumbal and South Sea Islander woman Amy McQuire writes:

> Their wounds also testify to this violence. But while this footage has been important for mobilising Aboriginal people, non-Indigenous Australia is still complacent and apathetic. They are not 'outraged' because they are not 'shocked'. There is nothing shocking about racist violence perpetrated by police, because it is normalised.

When we do hear about the Indigenous lives lost in custody, it is undoubtedly because of the persistence, expertise and courage of the families and communities who mourn them. But it is not enough to hear about justice – justice must be done.

Editor's note: At the time of editing (18 June 2021), the number of Aboriginal deaths in custody stands at 475.

Women are (rightly) angry. Now they need a plan

Michelle Arrow
Professor of History, Macquarie University

5 March 2021

Australian women have been most effective, politically, when they have harnessed their collective rage and turned it into action. They need to do it again now.

Like many Australians, I was delighted when activist Grace Tame was named the 2021 Australian of the Year. Tame is a powerful advocate for survivors of child sexual abuse, drawing on her own experience of being groomed and abused by a paedophile when she was just fifteen.

Tame's case was the catalyst for the creation of the #LetHerSpeak Tasmania campaign, which was created by journalist Nina Funnell in partnership with Marque Lawyers and End Rape On Campus Australia to overhaul gag laws that silenced victims of sexual abuse.

Accepting her award, Tame declared she was: 'using my voice, amongst a growing chorus of voices that will not be silenced. Let's make some noise, Australia.'

Tame's bravery inspired former political staffer Brittany Higgins to make some noise of her own. The revelation of her alleged sexual assault in a ministerial office and subsequent treatment by her employers has appalled observers.

Most recently, it has been alleged a man who is now a federal cabinet minister (revealed on Wednesday to be Attorney-General Christian Porter) raped a sixteen-year-old girl in 1988. The response that best reveals the prevailing political culture was when Prime Minister Scott Morrison, who was sent a letter outlining the allegation, airily admitted he hadn't read it. He added that because the minister has 'vigorously denied' the allegation, there were 'no matters' that required his attention.

In a defiant press conference on Wednesday, Porter denied the allegations. He refused to call for an inquiry or stand aside from his role, saying, 'If I stand down from my position as Attorney-General because of an allegation about something that simply did not happen, then any person in Australia can lose their career, their job, their life's work based on nothing more than an accusation that appears in print.'

To say Australian women are angry about the events of the past few weeks is an understatement. In a powerhouse address to the National Press Club on Wednesday, Tame stressed the importance of turning that rage into action: 'One voice, your voice, and our collective voices can make a difference. We are on the precipice of a revolution whose call to action needs to be heard loud and clear.'

Australian women's collective rage is not without precedent.

The women's movement of the 1970s was born, in part, out of anger. Women were angry they couldn't always control their fertility, or parent their own children. They were angry they were paid less than men for the same jobs. They were angry childcare was hard to access. And, frankly, they were angry at men. Activist and writer Kate Jennings articulated this rage in a speech at an anti-war rally in 1970:

> There are a lot of people who feel strongly about the Vietnam war. But how many of you, who can see so clearly the suffering and misery in Vietnam ... how many of you would get off your fat piggy asses and protest against the killing and victimisation of women in your own country.

The women's movement drew strength from talking. Sharing their experiences in consciousness-raising groups, women realised their problems were not personal but structural, demanding structural solutions.

It didn't take long for the movement to articulate its core demands: free abortion and childcare, equal pay, equal job opportunities and an end to media sexism. While they did not limit themselves to activism on these issues, they focused and shaped their work.

By early 1972, the Women's Electoral Lobby (WEL), the movement's moderate wing, ingeniously placed women's issues on the political agenda by inaugurating their candidate survey. WEL members in every Australian electorate interviewed all political candidates. Not only did the survey train women in political lobbying, it laid bare the views of the (mostly) male candidates on women's issues. It also gave women a political voice.

When Gough Whitlam's government was elected, in part because of WEL's advocacy, the women's movement used its new leverage to achieve reforms on equal pay and contraception, and later made important gains in childcare, the funding of women's refuges, and family law.

Whitlam appointed to his staff a women's affairs adviser, Elizabeth Reid, who worked to make government more responsive to women's needs. She, and subsequent feminists working inside the state, could not have exerted the influence they did without an active women's movement agitating for change.

Surprisingly, violence against women was not initially a primary focus of the women's movement. It emerged through consciousness raising and so too did feminist methods of addressing it: rape crisis centres and women's refuges.

Activism around sexual violence moved to centre stage: from 1978, Australian women marched against male sexual violence in Reclaim the Night marches, and in the early 1980s feminists marched on Anzac Day 'in memory of all women raped in all wars'.

Today, feminists are still campaigning against male violence against women. Over the past few years, we have mourned hundreds of women who have died due to family violence. We have witnessed royal commissions into family violence and into institutional responses to child sexual abuse. We have admired the courage of survivors like Rosie Batty. We gasped as serial sexual predators were exposed under the banner of #MeToo. But too little has actually changed.

Women are angry and they are tired. Tired of mansplainers and misogynists, and those who bleat #NotAllMen instead of asking #WhySoManyMen? Tired of women who have benefited from feminism yet refuse the label of 'feminist'. And tired of having to once again fight the battles that women in the 1970s and 1980s thought they had won.

Rage is politically potent, and useful. You only need to look at the ways Donald Trump fuelled his army of supporters to understand that. But if the lessons of second-wave feminism are any guide, women not only need to get angry, they need to get organised.

The women's movement was energised by its collective nature and common goals. Today's female rage is fierce, but it is not yet harnessed to a clear agenda for action. Women need to create this agenda together, and then work out how best to achieve it.

We know so much more about women's oppression today than women did in the 1970s, especially the ways in which different types of discrimination overlap and combine. We are perhaps more sceptical of the ability of institutions to effect change. And we are painfully aware neoliberalism has shrunk the state and limited the possibilities for activism.

But our scepticism, and our lack of attention, has exacted a cost. In the 1980s, government policy was routinely audited for its impact on women. But in the 1990s, feminist policy 'machinery' was steadily dismantled.

Today's Office for Women has a tiny staff and a low profile. It was not consulted on any of the major COVID-related policy shifts, like JobKeeper or changes to superannuation.

If our parliament is full of men who ignore, belittle and disrespect women, and women who enable these men, it is because we, the voters, have put them there. But we can also vote them out.

A women's candidate survey, ready to roll out at the next federal election, is just one strategy from the women's movement of the 1970s that might be worth reviving today. Women need to maintain their rage, but they need to turn it into political action too.

The death of bin Laden doesn't mean the terror threat is over

Michael Humphrey
Professor of Sociology and Social Policy, University of Sydney

5 May 2011

The US military's assassination of Osama bin Laden in North Pakistan is an important landmark in the 'war on terror'. As the leader of al Qaeda he was the primary target of the military campaign to defeat global Islamist insurgency. But his death ten years after 9/11, while important, does not defeat global jihadist terror.

9/11 changed the world. There was the immediate global impact of the attacks as an awesome spectacle and lives lost. Then there was the longer-term consequences of the 'war on terror'. President George Bush's declaration that 'you are either with us or against us' divided the world into friends and enemies, and Muslims into good and bad ones.

Miltary action

The 'war on terror' saw the invasion of Afghanistan, and then Iraq, to stop further terrorism, and intensified homeland security to prevent further attacks in the West.

It also greatly expanded transnational coordination and cooperation to hunt terrorists and police Muslim societies and communities abroad and in the West.

The 'war on terror' did not shrink the international jihadist political project but expanded it geographically, reaching into Muslim communities in the West.

Recruitment to radicalisation

9/11 recruited enthusiastic and inspired young Muslims to the global jihadist cause feeding on existing anti-Western and anti-American sentiment in the Muslim world.

It also alienated Muslims through their experience of becoming suspects and targets of 'war on terror' in Muslim countries invaded to defeat jihadist terrorism. In the West they were seen as potential recruits to global jihadist terrorism.

Guantanamo Bay and Abu Ghraib became synonymous with Muslim humiliation and injustice at the hands of the US for much of the Islamic world.

The bombings of London public transport in July 2005 were seen as a code for the menacing threat of 'homegrown' terrorism for Western countries, Australia included.

Muslims in the West were told the 'war on terror' was not against Islam. However, their experience of homeland security did not reassure them.

The West judges Islam

The view of Muslims as transnational risks, anti-terrorism laws that targeted them as suspicious, and government by the politics of fear of Muslims turned them into marginal citizens.

They were judged to be 'good' or 'bad' Muslims on the basis of their conformity with Western constructions of 'moderate' Islam. The veil, Islamic clerics and Islamic organisations have increasingly been policed as signs or sources of dangerous politicisation and even radicalisation. Muslim immigration to the West slowed and Islamphobia grew.

The influence of bin Laden

Osama bin Laden was the symbolic leader of the global Islamist jihadist project. He tapped into a longstanding Muslim anxiety about religious decline, and the contemporary Muslim experience of cultural crisis engendered by globalisation as westernisation.

Bin Laden inspired many Muslims, as a religious warrior fighting imperialism in Muslim countries, first Soviet imperialism and then American imperialism.

He will no doubt be seen by many Muslims as a martyr for the cause of the purification and revival of Islam and Muslim territories through violence.

But he was not the leader of a global Islamic organisation, party or army.

The al Qaeda franchises are loosely networked and trading on the prestige of the brand.

The global jihadist project is organised horizontally and not vertically. It is a project that exists in the belief there will be a transformation in society, and yet, its goals are ill-defined.

Democratic uprisings

The recent Arab 'Spring', propelled by unarmed citizen protest against entrenched authoritarian governments in the Arab world, is probably more significant in determining the fate of global jihadist terrorism than the death of Osama bin Laden.

This democratic politics of the street is the antithesis of the utopian and violent politics of the global jihad. Ironically, Muslims alienated in the West who have not understood the change in political mood and street protest in their home societies may still feel more connected to the globalised Islam and vulnerable to the sirens of the virtualised global jihad.

If the democratic impetus for change in the Arab world offers hope for the marginalisation of global jihadist violence, then the West needs to reciprocate by changing the security lens through which it has militarised the way we see our globalised world.

It has eroded our national perspective, undermined an earlier imagination of multiculturalism and joined us up to a transnational security project.

We urgently need to reassess our current social imagination, and how globalised cultural difference can be lived with and not become a mode of governance to divide according to risk classifications.

The *Herald Sun*'s Serena Williams cartoon draws on a long and damaging history of racist caricature

Clare Corbould
Associate Professor, Deakin University

11 September 2018

In the aftermath of the dramatic US Open women's final between Serena Williams and Naomi Osaka, Australian tabloid *Herald Sun* cartoonist Mark Knight sketched a cartoon of Williams that has drawn opprobrium worldwide.

Critics such as writer JK Rowling and basketball player Ben Simmons have denounced it as racist and sexist. However, the *Herald Sun's* editor, Damon Johnston, defended Knight, saying the cartoon had 'nothing to do with gender or race'.

But whether Knight and his editor realise it or not, the cartoon draws on at least 200 years of racist and sexist caricaturing of African and African-descended women.

Early cartoon caricatures

In the United States, the tradition of racist caricature began as slavery came to end. This was not a coincidence.

The first place to outlaw slavery in the newly formed United States was Vermont in 1777. Over the next fifty years, northern states abolished slavery at different rates. Then, in 1861, the nation went to war over slavery, and with the Union's victory four years later, this dark period of the nation's history officially came to a close.

But wealthy whites' desire for cheap labour did not end. In order to maintain a permanent underclass of workers, new and pernicious forms of racial classifications emerged. These were designed to keep Black people 'in their place' or prevent them from becoming 'uppity'.

The 19th century also saw the solidifying of now-discredited forms of science that pegged races to a so-called ladder of civilisation. White people, in this logic, had ascended to the top of the ladder. In the United States, African-descended people were at the bottom. (In Australia, white people pegged Aboriginal people to the bottom rung.)

Alongside such ideas came new ways to represent – or misrepresent – groups of people in imagery. Racist and sexist caricaturing became a staple of newspapers and pamphlets, which were circulating ever more cheaply by the decade. This was 'racism's visual vocabulary', to use a phrase coined by American history professor Martha S Jones.

American cartoonists exaggerated the features, clothes, speech and deportment of Black people. The effect, as in Edward Clay's famed 'Life in Philadelphia' series, was to suggest that African-Americans would never fit into city life as free people. Such stereotypes helped undermine free Black people's claim to citizenship and to rights as fundamental as the vote.

Stereotypes of Black people took several forms. Zip Coon was a dandy who imperfectly mimicked modern city ways and never earned an honest dollar; the 'mammy' existed only to take care of white people; harmless 'uncles' or 'sambos' were not very bright and good only for menial labour.

Cartoons often infantilised Black people into odd-looking, overgrown 'picaninnies', similar to Knight's depiction of Williams in his cartoon.

Damaging stereotypes of hyper-sexed Black characters emerged too, including the 'buck' and 'Jezebel'. These served as yet another way to control Black lives and labour.

Minstrels and film

Caricatures also extended beyond cartoons to what was fast becoming the most popular form of entertainment in the 19th century United States: blackface minstrelsy. Audiences across the country, and eventually all over the world (including Australia), revelled in this new comic form. Sharing a laugh by making fun of Black people became one way that white Americans united with large new groups of immigrants.

The idea that African-descended people were somehow less human or less advanced also enabled white people of different classes to feel united and superior to Black people. This feeling of superiority is what Black intellectual and activist WEB Du Bois called 'a psychological wage'.

It helped wealthy white people suppress alliances between poor white people and Black people who had been enslaved, or their descendants.

Racist caricaturing was so useful to those in power that by the end of the 19th century it was everywhere. Consumer goods, an ever-expanding market, were sold with images of caring Aunt Jemima and benign Uncle Ben (the latter is still on grocery shelves in Australia today, albeit with an updated image).

Such caricaturing continued to demean African-Americans into the 20th century. Some of the very first short films and feature films in the United States centred on Black characters who were stereotyped as lazy, thieving and/or stupid. *The Jazz Singer,* the first 'talkie', released in 1927, featured Al Jolson in blackface singing a song called 'Mammy'.

Right into my childhood in regional Australia, racial caricatures could be seen on TV's *The Bugs Bunny Show,* while more recent examples include Eddie Murphy's donkey in *Shrek* (2001) and *The Lion King*'s hyenas (1994).

The purpose of racist caricature of African-Americans is no longer to maintain a cheap workforce. It is also vital to note the ways African-Americans have resisted, negotiated and minimised harm wherever possible. But such images do continue to perpetuate racist myths about Black people's natures and capabilities, with other deleterious effects. They have had a long, damaging history, and it's time that 21st century media outlets such as the *Herald Sun* let them go.

Christchurch mosque shootings must end New Zealand's innocence about right-wing terrorism

Paul Spoonley
Pro Vice-Chancellor, College of Humanities and Social Sciences, Massey University

15 March 2019

Mosques across New Zealand remain closed and police presence is strong, following a terrorist attack at two mosques in central Christchurch on Friday.

Fifty people have been killed at Masjid Al Noor and a second mosque nearby.

Three people have been taken into custody in connection with the shootings. One man in his late twenties has been charged with murder.

In the hours after the attacks, New Zealand's Prime Minister, Jacinda Ardern, made it clear this was a terrorist attack of 'extraordinary and unprecedented violence' that had no place in New Zealand.

She said extremist views were not welcome and contrary to New Zealand values, and did not reflect New Zealand as a nation: 'It is one of New Zealand's darkest days. Many of the people affected by this act of extreme violence will be from our refugee and migrant communities. New Zealand is their home. They are us.'

She is right. Public opinion surveys such as the Asia New Zealand Foundation annual surveys of attitudes tend to show that a majority of New Zealanders are in favour of diversity and see immigration, in this case from Asia, as providing various benefits for the country.

But extremist politics, including the extreme nationalist and white supremacist politics that appear to be at the core of this attack on Muslims, have been part of our community for a long time.

History of white supremacy

I completed research in the UK on the National Front and British National Party in the late 1970s. When I returned to New Zealand, I was told explicitly, including by authorities that were charged with monitoring extremism, that we did not have similar groups here. But it did not take me long to discover quite the opposite.

Through the 1980s, I looked at more than seventy local groups that met the definition of being extreme right wing. The city that hosted many of these groups was Christchurch.

They were a mixture of skinhead, neo-Nazi and extreme nationalist groups. Some were traditional in their ideology, with a strong underpinning of anti-Semitism and a belief in the supremacy of the 'British race'. Others inverted the arguments of Māori nationalism to argue for separatism to keep the 'white race pure'.

And yes, there was violence. There was the 1989 shooting of an innocent bystander, Wayne Motz, in Christchurch by a skinhead, who then walked to a local police kiosk and shot himself. The pictures of the internment showed his friends giving Nazi salutes. In separate incidents, a Korean backpacker and a gay man were killed for ideological reasons.

Things have changed. The 1990s provided the internet and then social media. And events such as the September 11 terror attacks shifted the focus – anti-Semitism was now supplemented by Islamophobia.

Hate speech online

The Christchurch and Canterbury earthquakes and subsequent rebuild have significantly transformed the ethnic demography of Christchurch and made it much more multicultural – and more positive about that diversity. It is ironic that terrorism should take place in this city, despite its history of earlier far right extremism.

We tend not to think too much about the presence of racist and white supremacist groups, until there is some public incident like the desecration of Jewish graves in an Auckland cemetery or a march of black-shirted men (they are mostly men) asserting their 'right to be white'. Perhaps we are comfortable in thinking, as the Prime Minister has said, they are not part of our nation.

Last year, as part of a project to examine hate speech, I looked at what some New Zealanders were saying online. It did not take long to discover the presence of hateful and anti-Muslim comments. It would be wrong to characterise these views and comments as widespread, but New Zealand was certainly not exempt from Islamophobia.

Every so often, it surfaced, such as in the 2017 attack on a Muslim woman and her friends in a Huntly carpark, by a woman hurling cans and racist abuse.

An end to collective innocence

It became even more obvious during 2018. The Canadian YouTuber Stefan Molyneux sparked a public debate about his right to free speech, when he applied for a visa to visit New Zealand for a speaking tour with Lauren Southern, fellow Canadian YouTuber and white nationalist. Much of the public comment seemed to either overlook or condone his extreme views on what he regards as the threat posed by Islam.

And then there was the public protest in favour of free speech that occurred at the same time, and the signs warning us about the arrival of Sharia law or declaiming 'Free Tommy'. The latter refers to Tommy Robinson, a long-time activist and former leader of the English Defence League, who was sentenced to prison – and then released on appeal – for contempt of court, essentially by targeting Muslims before the courts.

There is plenty of evidence of local Islamophobic views, especially online. There are, and have been for a long time, individuals and groups who hold white supremacist views. They tend to threaten violence; seldom have they acted on those views. There is also a naivety among New Zealanders, including the media, about the need to be tolerant towards the intolerant.

There is not necessarily a direct causation between the presence of Islamophobia and what has happened in Christchurch. But this attack must end our collective innocence.

No matter the size of these extremist communities, they always represent a threat to our collective wellbeing. Social cohesion and mutual respect need to be asserted and continually worked on.

Editor's note: In 2020 the Christchurch mosque killer pleaded guilty to murdering fifty-one people and was sentenced to life in prison without parole – the first person in the country's history to receive the sentence.

The Anzac legend has blinded Australia to its war atrocities. It's time for a reckoning

Martin Crotty
Associate Professor in Australian History, University of Queensland

Carolyn Holbrook
ARC DECRA Fellow at Deakin University

7 December 2020

For years, Australians have faced a steady stream of investigative media reports about atrocities allegedly committed by the country's most elite soldiers in Afghanistan.

Yet, nothing could have prepared the nation for the breathtaking contents of the landmark report by Major General Paul Brereton into the actions of special forces, released last month after a four-year investigation. The reaction across Australia was one of horror and disbelief.

The inquiry found credible evidence to support allegations that thirty-nine Afghan civilians were illegally killed by Australian soldiers, some having weapons planted on them to make them appear to have been combatants.

Prisoners were shot for reasons as obtuse as saving the need for a second helicopter trip. Others were allegedly killed in a practice known as 'blooding', in which new soldiers were encouraged to achieve their first 'kill'. In one particularly appalling incident, special forces allegedly slit the throats of two fourteen-year-old boys and dumped their bodies in a river.

For most Australians, this is more than just rogue soldiers being found out for despicable behaviour. The depth of revulsion felt by many reflects the special place the country reserves for its armed forces, who have come to personify all that is best about Australia.

Where the Anzac legend originated

Military history sits at the heart of the Australian national identity – most visibly through the Anzac legend.

The word 'Anzac' is an acronym for Australian and New Zealand Army Corps. It was coined during the early phases of World War I, when Australians and New Zealanders were part of an allied force that landed at Gallipoli in modern-day Turkey in April 1915.

The invasion, devised by Britain's First Lord of the Admiralty, Winston Churchill, was unsuccessful in its goal of reaching Constantinople and knocking the Ottoman Empire out of the war.

But the young Australian nation, federated in 1901, took from the failed campaign a mythology of national birth.

Australia had been created during an age of elevated propaganda about empire, monarchy and the glory of battle. War was held to be the truest test of the character of men and nations.

In this era of 'new imperialism', the peaceful union of Australia's six British colonies carried a taint of illegitimacy because no blood had been spilled (the frontier wars with Aboriginal peoples did not count). The British journalist Alfred Buchanan wrote in 1907 that he

> pitied the little Australian [...] looking to nourish the flame of patriotic sentiment, [for ...] the altar has not been stained with crimson as every rallying centre of a nation should be.

So, by World War I, it was believed that a good showing in battle would expunge the convict stain and prove Australians worthy members of the British Empire.

This is why the date of the Gallipoli invasion, 25 April, quickly became Australia's most sacred national day. The young nation was drenched by a tide of khaki nationalism that has ebbed and flowed ever since.

War memorials and monuments were raised in towns and cities around the country, where citizens still gather each Anzac Day to engage in the rituals of what the late historian Ken Inglis called Australia's 'civil religion'.

How the Anzacs continue to be revered

Beginning in the 1990s, Australian politicians have also consciously and cleverly linked this nostalgia-tinted history to the work of the modern and highly professionalised Australian Defence Force. When the honour of Australia's revered soldiers is questioned, so too is the national self-image.

For example, *Beyond Compliance*, a 2011 report into the culture and personal conduct of members of the Defence Force, prompted by accusations of sexual harassment and other indiscretions, noted the Anzac legend provided an exemplar for the current military.

Similarly, in his 2015 dawn service speech on the centenary of the Gallipoli landings, then Prime Minister Tony Abbott lauded the Anzacs for their qualities of compassion, perseverance and mateship. In reverential tones, Abbott called them the 'founding heroes of modern Australia', and said they set an example for modern day Australians to follow: 'Yes, they are us; and when we strive enough for the right things, we can be more like them.'

Poignantly, Ben Roberts-Smith, Australia's most decorated contemporary soldier and among the men accused of war atrocities in Afghanistan, has also drawn inspiration from the Anzac legend. Roberts-Smith has said that Gallipoli is 'a big part of who we are as Aussies' and reflected on his boyhood fascination with the Anzacs: 'While other boys had posters of sporting heroes, I had posters of soldiers.'

A history of misconduct in war

But the idealisation of this Anzac history has always required Australians to turn a blind eye to uncomfortable truths.

Australian soldiers in World War I killed prisoners, deserted in record numbers, caught venereal disease at phenomenal rates and outperformed all other Western Front forces in causing trouble. In the World War II, Australians were often reluctant to take Japanese prisoners, choosing to illegally bayonet or shoot them instead. And Australian soldiers are known to have committed atrocities alongside their American counterparts in Vietnam, including 'bloodings' and 'throwdowns' (planting weapons on civilians after they were killed).

In recent years, we have become increasingly reluctant to see our Anzacs as killers, even when such killing is legitimate on military grounds. As represented most famously in Peter Weir's 1981 film, *Gallipoli*, the Anzac legend has become less about the combat ability of Australian soldiers and more about their suffering. It is war commemoration stripped down and refitted for the age of post-traumatic stress disorder.

The Anzacs that our nation so often lauds are fictional creations, shorn of the malevolence and downright murderous behaviour they frequently exhibited.

The alleged SAS atrocities do not fit this kinder, gentler version of the legend. They upend the way Australians like to imagine their armed forces, and by implication, themselves.

Tethering war to national self-image

We see two possibilities for how the current crisis will play out. The first is, the alleged war crimes will slowly be forgotten, just as previous atrocities have been.

There are already signs this is happening. Prime Minister Scott Morrison last week said he remained 'incredibly proud' of the ADF and emphasised that the alleged crimes were committed by 'a small number in a very big defence force'. He maintained the reputation of the broader defence force would be unaffected.

The other possibility is Australia will adopt a more realistic attitude towards its soldiers and the conflicts they fight in. These conflicts are complex, and rarely conducted without some descent into the moral abyss. Some of our soldiers are not good people, and those that are good are capable of lapses. War is an ugly business, and we pay a price for tethering it so tightly to our national self-image.

As historians of Australia's war experiences, we hope and wish for a national reckoning about our record of war atrocities. But as historians of Anzac, we anticipate that the great mythological behemoth will barely sway from its course in the face of these allegations.

Editor's note: Roberts-Smith has denied the allegations of wrongdoing and, at the time of editing, is pursuing legal action against Nine mastheads, claiming to have been defamed.

Why children are prime targets of armed groups in northern Nigeria

Hakeem Onapajo
Senior Lecturer in the Department of Political Science and International Relations, Nile University of Nigeria

16 March 2021

Due to growing insecurity, Nigeria is gradually becoming one of the most dangerous places to live. The 2020 Global Terrorism Index identified the country as the third most affected by terrorism. There was a sharp increase in Boko Haram's targeting of civilians, by 25 per cent, and killings by herdsmen increased by 26 per cent, compared with the previous year. The two countries higher on the index are Iraq and Afghanistan.

According to the Nigeria Security Tracker, 2769 violent deaths were recorded between February 2020 and February 2021 in Borno State alone. Similarly, ransom-kidnapping by armed groups has increased substantially in the past five years. Over $18 million was paid as ransom for kidnapped victims between 2011 and 2020.

While insecurity is common in Nigeria, the northern region has been most affected. This is due to Boko Haram attacks, banditry, farmers–herdsmen conflicts, kidnappings and ethno-religious conflicts. Sadly, children have not been spared.

In the north-east, children have been murdered, abducted and used as sex slaves, forcefully recruited as child soldiers, and suffer from diseases and malnutrition at the internally displaced persons camps. The United

Nations says almost 4000 children were killed in only a year, 2015 to 2016. UNICEF reported that an estimated 1.9 million people are displaced – and about 60 per cent of them are children; many under the age of five. The rising phenomenon has further manifested in the recent wave of attacks on schools and kidnapping of students.

My article 'Children in Boko Haram conflict: The neglected facet of a decade of terror in Nigeria', published last year, highlights why children have become targets for the armed groups in northern Nigeria. This paper focuses on children in the Boko Haram conflict, which has for over ten years ravaged the north-eastern part of Nigeria and around Lake Chad.

Despite the reality that children have increasingly become the face of insecurity in northern Nigeria, the literature has been silent on issues related to child security. My study therefore aimed to address the perspective of children in the conflict.

I found that children were of strategic interest to both the terrorists and the state security forces. I concluded child security had not been given sufficient attention in Nigeria and should be included in peace-building efforts in north-eastern Nigeria.

Children and conflict in northern Nigeria

The dimension of children in violent conflicts in northern Nigeria gained momentum in 2013, when Boko Haram adopted the strategy of direct attacks on schools, hospitals and centres for internally displaced people.

It started with the midnight raid of a dormitory in Gujba, Yobe State, leading to the murder of forty-four schoolboys by the terrorist group in September 2013. Five months later, another boarding school was attacked, and fifty-nine boys were murdered in the same state. In April 2014, 276 schoolgirls were abducted in Chibok in Borno State.

UNICEF in its 2018 report said the group had kidnapped over 1000 children since 2013. Between 2015 and 2016, the UN estimated 3909 children were killed.

In the past five years, the rise of banditry added a new and dangerous dimension to attacks on children. On 11 December 2020, 333 students were kidnapped in Kankara, Katsina State. On 20 December 2020, eighty students at an Islamic school were kidnapped in Mahuta, Katsina State. Twenty-seven students were abducted in Kagara, Niger State, on 17 February 2021.

The latest occurred on 25 February, with the abduction of 317 schoolgirls in Jangebe, Talata Mafara Local Government area, Zamfara State.

Why children are prime targets

Our study used a qualitative approach, relying on data from institutional reports of intergovernmental agencies like the United Nations, United Nations Children's Fund and the International Organization for Migration; non-governmental agencies like Human Rights Watch, Amnesty International, Global Coalition to Protect Education from Attack, Mercy Corps and Open Doors, and media reports.

The research showed that children were of strategic interest to the armed groups for many reasons. First, targeting children proved effective as a tool to negotiate for the release of members of the group in prison, and to receive huge ransoms to purchase weapons and fund their operations.

Second, the armed groups were interested in children as a way to gain local and international attention to show their strength, seek international collaborations with similar groups and amplify their demands to the state authorities.

Third, children were useful for their military operations, especially for terrorist groups. They could plant explosives, act as human shields or suicide bombers, and spy on the other parties because they didn't arouse suspicion.

Fourth, the attack on schools corresponded with the central ideology driving terrorism in the region, which was based on opposition to Western education. The increased attacks showed the plan was to make the region insecure for teaching and learning.

Fifth, girls were of interest to the armed groups for sexual exploitation. Abducted girls were sometimes raped or forced into marriages in the camps.

Nigeria must safeguard its children more

Child security has not been given sufficient attention in Nigeria. This explains the successful attacks on children in recent times. Child security underscores the essence of the United Nations Convention on the Rights of the Child, which Nigeria is a party to.

The government must show serious commitment to children's security by tackling the rising problem of insecurity ravaging the country.

The paper underscores the need for specialised programs that can address the peculiar challenges of children's involvement in the conflict zones and not merely incorporate them into adult-focused or general programs.

The international community, including important non-governmental organisations promoting children's rights and welfare, must also compel the authorities to secure the children and internationalise the problem of child insecurity in Nigeria.

PART IV

On health and life

How long does sex normally last?

Brendan Zietsch
ARC Future Fellow, University of Queensland

4 April 2016

If you're a non-scientist, you might have once asked yourself, propped against the bedhead after disappointingly quick intercourse, how long does sex 'normally' last?

A scientist, though, would phrase the same question in an almost comically obscure way: *What is the mean intravaginal ejaculation latency time?*

I know there's a lot more to sex than putting the penis into the vagina and ejaculating, but the rest is not always easy to define. (Kissing? Rubbing? Grinding?) To keep things simple and specific, we'll just focus on the time to ejaculation.

Measuring an average time to ejaculation is not a straightforward matter. *What about just asking people how long they take?* you say. Well, there are two main problems with this. One is that people are likely to be biased upwards in their time estimates, because it's socially desirable to say you go long into the night.

The other problem is that people don't necessarily know how long they go for. Sex isn't something people normally do while monitoring the bedside clock, and unassisted time estimation may be difficult during a transportative session of lovemaking.

What does the research say?

'A multinational population survey of intravaginal ejaculation latency time' (Marcel D Waldinger et al.) is the best study we have estimating the average time to ejaculation in the general population. It involved 500 couples from around the world timing themselves having sex over a four-week period – using a stopwatch.

That is as practically awkward as it sounds: participants pressed 'start' at penile penetration and 'stop' at ejaculation. You may note this could affect the mood somewhat, and perhaps not exactly reflect the natural flow of things. But – science is rarely perfect, and this is the best we've got.

So, what did the researchers find? The most striking result is that there was a huge amount of variation. The average time for each couple (that is, averaged across all the times they had sex) ranged from thirty-three seconds to forty-four minutes. That's an eighty-fold difference.

It's clear, then, there's no one 'normal' amount of time to have sex. The average (median, technically) across all couples, though, was 5.4 minutes. This means that if you line up the 500 couples from shortest sex to longest sex, the middle couple goes for an average of 5.4 minutes each time they do it.

There were some interesting secondary results too. For example, condom use didn't seem to affect the time taken, and neither did men's being circumcised or not, which challenges some conventional wisdom regarding penile sensitivity and its relationship to staying power in the sack.

It didn't much matter which country the couples came from either – unless they came from Turkey, in which case their sex tended to be significantly shorter (3.7 minutes) than that of couples from other countries (Netherlands, Spain, the United Kingdom, and the United States). Another surprising finding was that the older the couple, the shorter the sex, contrary to the prevailing wisdom (probably peddled by older men).

Why do we have sex for so long?

As an evolutionary researcher, all this talk of how long sex lasts make me wonder: *Why does it last any time at all?* All sex really needs to achieve, it seems, is to put sperm into the vagina. Why all the thrusting and bumping? Instead of sliding the penis in and out many hundreds of times per sexual session, why not just put it in once, ejaculate, and then go have a lemonade and get on with the rest of the day?

Before you say, *Because it's fun to go in and out!*, remember evolution doesn't care about fun per se – it generally only 'designs' things to be enjoyable if they helped our ancestors pass on their genes to future generations. For example, even though we like eating food, we don't chew each mouthful of it for five minutes just to make the enjoyment last longer. That would be inefficient, and so we've evolved to find it gross.

Why we last so long is a pretty complicated question with no clear answer, but a clue may be in the way the penis is shaped. In 2003, in

'The human penis as a semen displacement device', researchers showed – using artificial vaginas, artificial penises, and artificial sperm (corn syrup) – that the ridge around the head of the penis actually scoops out pre-existing syrup from the vagina.

What this suggests is that men's repeated thrusting might function to displace other men's semen before ejaculating, ensuring their own swimmers have a better chance of reaching the egg first. Incidentally, this could explain why it becomes painful for a man to continue thrusting after ejaculating, since that would risk scooping out his own semen as well.

What to do with this information? My advice would be to try not to think about it during the throes of passion.

Why bad moods are good for you: The surprising benefits of sadness

Joseph Paul Forgas
Scientia Professor of Psychology, UNSW

15 May 2017

Homo sapiens is a very moody species. Even though sadness and bad moods have always been part of the human experience, we now live in an age that ignores or devalues these feelings.

In our culture, normal human emotions like temporary sadness are often treated as disorders. Manipulative advertising, marketing and self-help industries claim happiness should be ours for the asking. Yet, bad moods remain an essential part of the normal range of moods we regularly experience.

Despite the near-universal cult of happiness and unprecedented material wealth, happiness and life satisfaction in Western societies have not improved for decades. (See, for example, 'Beyond money: Toward an economy of well-being' by Ed Diener and Martin EP Seligman.)

It's time to reassess the role of bad moods in our lives. We should recognise they are a normal, and even a useful and adaptive, part of being human, helping us cope with many everyday situations and challenges.

A short history of sadness

In earlier historical times, short spells of feeling sad or moody (known as mild dysphoria) were accepted as a normal part of everyday life. In fact, many of the greatest achievements of the human spirit deal with evoking, rehearsing and even cultivating negative feelings.

Greek tragedies exposed audiences to, and trained them to accept and deal with, the inevitable misfortune of human life. Shakespeare's tragedies are classics because they echo this theme. And the works of many great artists, such as Beethoven and Chopin in music, or Chekhov and Ibsen in literature, explore the landscape of sadness, a theme long recognised as instructive and valuable.

Ancient philosophers also believed accepting bad moods is essential to living a full life. Even hedonist philosophers, like Epicurus, recognised living well involves exercising wise judgement, restraint and self-control, and accepting inevitable adversity.

Other philosophers, like the Stoics, also highlighted the importance of learning to anticipate and accept misfortunes such as loss, sorrow or injustice.

What is the point of sadness?

Psychologists who study how our feelings and behaviours have evolved over time maintain all our affective states (such as moods and emotions) have a useful role: they alert us to states of the world we need to respond to.

In fact, the range of human emotions includes many more negative than positive feelings. Negative emotions such as fear, anger, shame or disgust are helpful because they assist us to recognise, avoid and overcome threatening or dangerous situations.

But what is the point of sadness, perhaps the most common negative emotion, and one most practising psychologists deal with?

Intense and enduring sadness, such as depression, is obviously a serious and debilitating disorder. However, mild, temporary bad moods may serve an important and useful adaptive purpose, by helping us to cope with everyday challenges and difficult situations.

These moods also act as a social signal that communicates disengagement and withdrawal from competition and provides a protective cover. When we appear sad or in a bad mood, people are often concerned and inclined to help.

Some negative moods, such as melancholia and nostalgia (a longing for the past), may even be pleasant, and seem to provide useful information to guide future plans and motivation.

Sadness can also enhance empathy, compassion, connectedness, and moral and aesthetic sensibility. And sadness has long been a trigger for artistic creativity. (See, for example, 'Feeling sad makes us more creative' by Jonah Lehrer.)

Recent scientific experiments document the benefits of mild bad moods (see, for example, 'Don't worry, be sad! On the cognitive, motivational, and interpersonal benefits of negative mood' by Joseph P Forgas). These often work as automatic, unconscious alarm signals, promoting a more attentive and detailed thinking style. In other words, bad moods help us to be more attentive and focused in difficult situations.

In contrast, a positive mood (like feeling happy) typically serves as a signal indicating familiar and safe situations, and results in a less detailed and attentive processing style.

Psychological benefits of sadness

There is now growing evidence that negative moods, like sadness, have psychological benefits.

To demonstrate this, researchers first manipulate people's mood (by showing happy or sad films, for example), then measure changes in performance in various cognitive and behavioural tasks.

Feeling sad or in a bad mood produces a number of benefits:

- better memory: in one study, a bad mood (caused by bad weather) resulted in people better remembering the details of a shop they just left. (See 'Can bad weather improve your memory? An unobtrusive field study of natural mood effects on real-life memory' by Joseph P Forgas et al.) Bad mood can also improve eyewitness memories by reducing the effects of various distractions, such as irrelevant, false or misleading information;
- more accurate judgements: a mild bad mood also reduces some biases and distortions in how people form impressions. For instance, slightly sad judges formed more accurate and reliable impressions about others because they processed details more effectively. We found bad moods also reduced gullibility and increased scepticism when evaluating urban myths and rumours,

and even improved people's ability to detect deception more accurately. (See 'On being happy and gullible: Mood effects on skepticism and the detection of deception' by Joseph P Forgas et al.) People in a mild bad mood are also less likely to rely on simplistic stereotypes;

- motivation: other experiments found that when happy and sad participants were asked to perform a difficult mental task, those in a bad mood tried harder and persevered more. They spent more time on the task, attempted more questions and produced more correct answers;
- better communication: the more attentive and detailed thinking style promoted by a bad mood can also improve communication. We found people in a sad mood used more effective persuasive arguments to convince others, were better at understanding ambiguous sentences and communicated better when talking (see 'When sad is better than happy: Negative affect can improve the quality and effectiveness of persuasive messages and social influence strategies' by Joseph P Forgas);
- increased fairness: other experiments found a mild bad mood caused people to pay greater attention to social expectations and norms, and they treated others less selfishly and more fairly.

Counteracting the cult of happiness

By extolling happiness and denying the virtues of sadness, we set an unachievable goal for ourselves. We may also be causing more disappointment; some say, even depression. (See, for example, 'Does trying to be happy make us unhappy?' by Adam Grant.)

It is increasingly recognised that being in a good mood, despite some advantages, is not universally desirable.

Feeling sad or in a bad mood helps us to focus better on the situation we find ourselves in, and so increases our ability to monitor and successfully respond to more demanding situations.

These findings suggest the unrelenting pursuit of happiness may often be self-defeating. A more balanced assessment of the costs and benefits of good and bad moods is long overdue.

If feelings of sadness persist, contact your GP or other local support services.

Six myths about vaccination – and why they're wrong

Rachael Dunlop
Post-doctoral Fellow, University of Technology Sydney

26 April 2013

Recently released government figures show levels of childhood vaccination have fallen to dangerously low levels in some areas of Australia, resulting in some corners of the media claiming reignition of 'the vaccine debate'.

Well, scientifically, there's no debate. In combination with clean water and sanitation, vaccines are one of the most effective public health measures ever introduced, saving millions of lives every year.

Those who claim there is a 'debate' will cite a series of canards designed to scare people away from vaccinating, but if you're not familiar with their claims, you could easily be convinced by anti-vaccine rhetoric.

What is true and what is not?

Let's address just a few of the common vaccine myths and explain why they're wrong.

1. Vaccines cause autism

The myth that vaccines are somehow linked to autism is an unsinkable rubber duck. Initiated in 1998 following the publication of the now notorious *Lancet* paper, (not-a-Dr) Andrew Wakefield was the first to suggest that the measles mumps rubella (MMR) vaccine might be linked to autism.

What he didn't reveal was that he had multiple conflicts of interest, including that he was being paid by lawyers assembling a class action against the manufacturers of MMR, and that he himself had submitted an application for a patent for a single measles vaccine.

It eventually unravelled for Wakefield when the paper was retracted in 2010. He was struck from the medical register for behaviour classified as 'dishonest, unethical and callous' and the *British Medical Journal* accused him of deliberate fraud.

But once the idea was floated, scientists were compelled to investigate, particularly when it stood to impact public health so dramatically. One of the most powerful pieces of evidence to show there is no link between vaccines and autism comes from Japan, where the MMR was replaced with single vaccines mid-1993. (See 'Japanese study is more evidence that MMR does not cause autism' by Andrew Cole.) Guess what happened? Autism continued to rise.

After this door closed, anti-vaxxers shifted the blame to thiomersal, a mercury-containing component (not be confused with the scary type that accumulates in the body). Small amounts of thiomersal were used as a preservative in some vaccines, but this never included MMR.

Thiomersal, or ethyl-mercury, was removed from all scheduled childhood vaccines in 2000, so if it were contributing to rising cases of autism, you would expect a dramatic drop following its removal. Instead, like with the MMR in Japan, the opposite happened, and autism continues to rise.

Further evidence comes from a recently published exhaustive review examining 12,000 research articles covering eight different vaccines, which also concluded there was no link between vaccines and autism. (See *Adverse Effects of Vaccines: Evidence and Causality*, editors Kathleen Stratton et al.)

Yet, the myth persists and probably for several reasons, one being that the time of diagnosis for autism coincides with kids receiving several vaccinations and, also, we currently don't know what causes autism. But we do know what doesn't, and that's vaccines.

2. Smallpox and polio have disappeared so there's no need to vaccinate anymore

It's precisely because of vaccines that diseases such as smallpox have disappeared.

India recently experienced two years without a single case of polio because of a concerted vaccination campaign.

Australia was declared measles-free in 2005 by the World Health Organization (WHO) – before we stopped being so vigilant about vaccinating and outbreaks began to reappear.

The impact of vaccine complacency can be observed in the current measles epidemic in Wales, where there are now over 800 cases and has been one death, and many people presenting are of the age who missed out on MMR vaccination following the Wakefield scare.

In many ways, vaccines are a victim of their own success, leading us to forget just how debilitating preventable diseases can be – not seeing kids in calipers or hospital wards full of iron lungs means we forget just how serious these diseases can be.

3. More vaccinated people get the disease than the unvaccinated

Although this sounds counterintuitive, it's actually true, but it doesn't mean that vaccines don't work, as anti-vaxxers will conflate it. Remember that no vaccine is 100 per cent effective and vaccines are not a force-field. So, while it's still possible to get the disease you've been vaccinated against, disease severity and duration will be reduced.

With pertussis (whooping cough), for example, severe complications such as pneumonia and encephalitis (brain inflammation) occur almost exclusively in the unvaccinated.

Therefore, since the majority of the population is vaccinated, it follows that most people who get a particular disease will be vaccinated, but, critically, they will suffer fewer complications and long-term effects than those who are completely unprotected.

4. My unvaccinated child should be of no concern to your vaccinated one

Vaccination is not just a personal issue, it's a community responsibility, largely because of a concept known as 'community immunity'. This describes a level of vaccination that prevents epidemics or outbreaks from taking hold and spreading.

Some people question the validity of this concept, sometimes referred to as herd immunity, but the impact of it breaking down can be easily observed in places where vaccination levels fall dangerously low – take the current measles outbreak in Wales, for example.

The other important factor about community immunity is it protects those who, for whatever reason, can't be vaccinated or are not fully vaccinated. This includes very young children, immunocompromised people (such as cancer sufferers) and elderly people.

5. Vaccines contain toxins

A cursory search of Google for vaccine ingredients pulls up a mishmash of scary-sounding ingredients that to the uninitiated can sound like 'franken-science'.

Some of these claims are patently untrue (there is no anti-freeze in vaccines) or are simple scaremongering (regarding the rumour of aborted foetuses, in the 1960s some cells were extracted from a foetus to establish a cell line that is still used in labs today). Some of the claimed chemicals (and, remember, everything is made of chemicals) are present, but are at such low levels as to never reach toxicity.

The simple thing to remember is the poison is in the dose – in high enough doses, even water can kill you. And there's fifty times more formaldehyde in a pear than in a vaccine.

Also, if you ever read the claim that 'vaccines are injected directly into the blood stream' (they're not), be sceptical of any other claims the writer is making.

6. Vaccines will overwhelm kids' undeveloped immune systems

The concept of 'too many too soon' was recently examined in a detailed analysis of the US childhood immunisation schedule by the Institute of Medicine (see *The Childhood Immunization Schedule and Safety: Stakeholder Concerns, Scientific Evidence, and Future Studies*). Experts specifically looked for evidence that vaccination was linked to 'autoimmune diseases, asthma, hypersensitivity, seizures, child developmental disorders, learning or developmental disorders, or attention deficit or disruptive disorders', including autism. The researchers confirmed the childhood vaccination schedule was safe.

The number of immune challenges (between 2000 to 6000) that children fight every day in the environment is significantly greater than the number of antigens or reactive particles in all their vaccinations combined (about 150 for the entire vaccination schedule).

The next time you hear these myths about vaccination, you'll hopefully have some evidence up your sleeve to debunk them.

An exclusive (and imaginary) interview with the coronavirus

Franck Courchamp
Research Director, CNRS, Université Paris-Saclay

25 November 2020

In this interview, Franck Courchamp, director of research at the CNRS and holder of the AXA Chair of Invasion Biology at the University of Paris-Saclay, puts himself in the place of the SARS-CoV-2 virus, which has infected nearly 60 million people worldwide and killed more than 1.4 million. In addition to its unexpected form, this interview also gave the author an opportunity to change our perspective on the stakes of the pandemic and the lessons it may hold for us.

Coronavirus, who are you?

I'd like to start by saying, in all modesty, that I am the king, and the name you gave me proves that – *corona* is Latin for 'crown'. Strangely enough, my very simplicity confuses you. You can't even decide whether or not I'm alive, and you're still wondering the same thing about all my fellow viruses.

Personally, I don't much care where you classify me. You could say I'm a sort of microscopic biological machine, with a very simple program: survive and reproduce in order to live on from one generation to the next. In that respect, I have exactly the same goal as any living species.

The fundamental difference is that I only need the bare minimum to achieve that goal: I just get into my host's cells, borrow whatever I need to keep operating, and hijack the cells' machinery to make copies of myself. I then release my clones – brand-new viral particles – and they set out in search of other cells to infect. We coronaviruses can produce a thousand copies of ourselves per infected cell in barely ten hours.

Yet, in spite of all that, I'm not big. My diameter is about 100 nanometers, or one 10,000th of a millimetre.

I'm a thousand times smaller than bacteria (which are ten to 100 times smaller than a human cell) – in other words, 50 trillion times smaller than a drop of water. A single one of your cells is way bigger to me than an immense city is to you.

Why do you infect people?

That's a strange question. Humans are my habitat, my ecosystem, my resources ... It's like me asking you why you live where you do – on a mountain, or a plain or wherever.

But I don't have a sedentary lifestyle like yours. I'm a nomad, because my vessels – the people or animals I infect – aren't immortal. To survive, I have to find a new host before the first one disappears. I admit we're sometimes responsible for their untimely demise, because the bodies of some of our hosts don't like it when we start proliferating. Others fall victim to the war their immune systems wage on us, which can sometimes spiral out of control.

How do you infect us?

I use simple means. You've already discovered some of my secrets – that I can travel in saliva and sneeze droplets, and I can stay on people's hands or on objects touched by hands.

I can squeeze inside a millilitre of saliva with 100 billion of my fellow coronaviruses and survive for five days on plastic, or a week on a surgical mask. I may not be very sophisticated, but I'm really efficient ... like all viruses, in fact. We're endlessly adaptable.

Consider the problem of spreading to another host. Luckily, you humans produce nasal mucus, especially when you're infected by one of us respiratory viruses. An infected person who sneezes is transformed into a powerful spraying machine that can transport us to our next victims at a speed of over 50 kilometres per hour, in a cloud of tens of thousands of droplets. These also end up on your hands, which you put all over the place. All this provides a very practical means of transport and helps us spread more easily.

Other viruses choose different fluids. For example, some of us give you diarrhoea, which results in highly efficient mass spreading. Others hang around in your seminal or vaginal fluid and spread when you have sex. You can isolate all you like, but, as a species, you have to reproduce at some point ...

Some viruses change their hosts' behaviour to spread more easily – like rabies, which causes confusion, aggression and a tendency to bite. And it's difficult to fight against that, isn't it?

Why do you viruses have it in for us humans?

Don't be so self-centred! We don't have it in for you – we neither love nor hate you. You just happen to be our favourite vessels and make things easier for us in so many ways. To start with, humans often live in densely populated places and their global population is interconnected, which makes potential hosts almost systematically available to us the world over.

I made that quite clear over the past year. After starting out from somewhere in China, I soon turned up on every continent and in the remotest corners of the planet – and I don't even have legs. Other animal populations are generally fragmented, limiting our chances of dispersal and confining us to small areas. But human beings are a whole other kettle of fish, so to speak. As the song goes, there's no mountain high enough, valley low enough, or river wide enough to keep us from getting to you. We travel from host to host by car, boat or plane: the world is our oyster. Given how restlessly humans move, you helped us create initial infection sites on every continent in less than a week.

What's more, humans keep a large part of their population in pretty deplorable sanitary conditions, which really helps us. Not to mention the behaviour of some of your leaders, who aren't ethical or intelligent enough to behave responsibly. This creates opportunities for us in some parts of the world, where the epidemic is downplayed or denied to avoid the problem of having to face up to it ...

But you didn't infect human beings at first ...

That's true. I used to depend on other animal species. However, by replicating over and over in the animals' infected cells, some clones mutate and become slightly different. And, from time to time, one of those mutants hits the jackpot: its mutation allows it to survive and spread via other animals than those its fellow viruses usually infect. Then you have a new strain of virus, ready to change host.

But it's not just a question of having the ability to infect a new animal species, you also have to get close enough to be able to infect it. The likelihood of those events coinciding is pretty small, but two factors work in our favour.

First, we're very, very numerous. For the 6500 or so mammalian species, there are about 320,000 different viruses that can infect mammals. And the more viruses, the more mutations.

Second, humans' many contacts with other species increase our chances of encountering and infecting you. And those opportunities are increasing, thanks to your intrusions into the territories of species that are already stressed by being hunted, deprived of their natural habitats and resources, and subjected to pollution or climate change. Then there are all the wild species you hunt, put in cages, pile up in markets and eat, sometimes improperly cooked, to the tune of millions of tons per year. That's how the HIV, SARS, Ebola, Zika and MERS viruses managed to infect you in recent years.

I might add that the result is pretty much the same when a virus infects a domesticated species rather than a human being. When you encroach on bats' territories and set up massive pig farms near their ruined habitats, you're increasing the chances a bat virus (such as the Nipah) will shift to the pigs that come into contact with bat saliva or excrement (which contain viruses). And as the pigs are crowded together and kept in wretched sanitary conditions, the chances of transmission increase and nothing can stop us.

Picture a bunch of stressed and sickly hosts, living in their own excrement among the corpses of their fellow creatures … it's an all-you-can-eat buffet for a virus. That's how swine flu and the H5N1 bird flu managed to infiltrate poultry and pig farms a few years ago. Concentrations of sickly hosts result in incredible concentrations of virus, which boosts our chances of spreading from domesticated animals to humans. Like the H5N1 or the Nipah (whose case fatality rate is 40 to 75 per cent in humans).

As I said before, my main problem is infecting the first human. Your globalisation system does the rest. It's as if you set it up to allow for the free circulation of viruses. So, thanks very much, *merci beaucoup*, *danke schön*, 衷心感谢, *muchas gracias*, большое спасибо, etc.

Do you realise the damage you do?

We mean you no more harm than a sheep does to a clump of grass. If we had any say in the matter, we'd obviously prefer our infected humans to stay alive and keep accommodating us indefinitely. But because our hosts sometimes die, we have to replicate quickly, so that we can infect another host before the first one disappears. This intense replication causes symptoms that can be harmful or even fatal. One of the problems is that if we just chill out and lie low, and if we don't find a good hiding place in your body, our initial small numbers risk being overcome by your immune systems. It's not easy to strike a balance between surviving without doing you too much harm and being totally wiped out.

Anyway, we viruses and the species we infect are usually linked by hundreds of thousands of years of coevolution and by now are relatively well 'adapted' to each other. Therefore, in the vast majority of cases, there's little damage on either side.

Above all, you mustn't forget that we viruses play an important regulatory role for other living populations (micro-organisms, plants, animals, etc.). If we all disappeared, they might end up overpopulating and using up all their resources, which would put them at risk of starving to death … Actually, we're said to be of major importance for the ecology and evolution of the living world.

What's more, a lot of viruses are beneficial to you. For instance, they kill certain bacteria that you're not too keen on either. Some researchers have even succeeded in using viruses instead of antibiotics to kill bacteria (see 'Viruses genetically engineered to kill bacteria rescue girl with antibiotic-resistant infection' by Alex Fox). And let's not forget that many viruses have what could be called a 'neutral' effect: in humans (since you're so self-centred), some 5000 different viruses have been discovered, but less than 3 per cent are 'pathogenic', i.e. the cause of an illness. Which is not very many, when you think about it.

Finally, there are all the viruses you're not interested in because they've shown so little interest in you. They're present in the soil, suspended in the air, floating in the water, and are in plants, insects, starfish ... For example, there are a million viruses suspended in 1 litre of seawater. In fact, there are so many viruses suspended in the oceans that, despite their ridiculously tiny size, they would stretch beyond our neighbouring galaxies if they were laid end to end.

As I've said, viruses are everywhere, even though you can't see them. Sometimes they're right in front of you and you don't even recognise them, like the amazing giant viruses, bigger than the bacteria scientists used to mistake them for (see 'Discovery of the giant Mimivirus' by David R Wessner).

Actually, where do you viruses come from?

I suppose you mean *when* do we come from? Well, as a matter of fact, we've always been around. Long before human beings ever existed, and long before even your oldest animal ancestors. Some people say we're older than the oldest bacteria. We were already present at the origin of life and have played a central role in evolution, particularly by allowing for gene transfer – not from one generation to the next, but between species. We're so old, some of us have integrated into human genomes and become a part of you.

In all, almost 10 per cent of the human genome is virus DNA, integrated into your chromosomes. And some of the new genes we viruses have given you are important, or even essential. In mammals, for example, the only reason the mother's immune system doesn't reject the embryo as a foreign body (a hybrid between the father and mother) is the existence of the placenta, which evolved from a virus integrated into your genome. Hey, don't worry about thanking us.

And what about you, coronavirus SARS-CoV-2? Where do you come from?

Which species did my ancestors infect before they moved on to you? I don't know. But does it matter whether they were bats, pangolins, monkeys or something else? What would you do if you found out? Would you stop poaching and eating that particular species? Would you wipe it out? Would you do the same to all the species whose viruses you might catch? That's obviously out of the question – there'd be hardly any animals left.

Anyway, why are you looking for culprits when it's obvious who they really are? Aren't the real ones the people who stir things up by upsetting virus–animal systems that had managed to remain pretty much self-contained for millions of years? If you tease a cat and it scratches you, will you eliminate all cats? Wouldn't it be better to stop pulling their tails?

How can we get rid of you?

In theory it's quite simple. You just need to think of an epidemic as a forest fire. Both are natural phenomena, but they can get out of control when you play with the laws of nature. Fires, for example, are fuelled by a combination of favourable conditions such as the accumulation of deadwood. After a strong initial blaze they generally die out when they occur in areas where the trees are too far apart for the flames to move from one to another (the equivalent of your social distancing), or where the tree species are less flammable (immunised against fire).

The situation is pretty much the same with natural epidemics. They appear, then keep spreading until contagion is slowed when the majority of infected people fail to contaminate others – because they don't encounter any (thanks to social distancing and quarantine), or because the people they meet have acquired immunity (during a previous infection or by vaccination). If the infection rate slows, the epidemic will fade out and eventually disappear.

So, what really matters most is learning how to avoid the next of your fellow viruses?

Yes indeed, because it's not a question of whether the next cross-species virus will threaten humans, but of *when*.

Will you be ready? You'll need to react quickly, because more and more epidemics have spread from wild animals in recent years, and your societies on several continents have already had a taste of some of my cousin viruses …

We emerging viruses have killed millions of humans, sometimes striking at random and sometimes targeting specific categories – the most physically vulnerable, in the present case. We've jeopardised your economic and political systems, locked you up in your homes in fear and prompted the craziest conspiracy theories. What lessons have you learned?

What do you have in store for us in the future?

I'd be hard put to answer that question: my numerous offspring and I infect and mutate at random. If you survive my presence in your body and recover, will you be immunised against my return? I don't know and don't care. Will you be able to keep me at a distance with your masks and your social distancing during the second wave or third wave? That's what we'll find out together.

One thing's for sure: I won't be exactly the same from one year to the next. Remember, we viruses mutate. And if we're very numerous – for example, when millions of humans are infected, which is the case at the moment – our mutations are more numerous too.

Most mutations result in less viable, less contagious or less virulent strains that soon die out. But, less frequently, mutations can lead to more contagious or deadlier strains. Although these more dangerous mutations are unusual among coronaviruses, the harder you find it to keep us in check, the more prolific we become, and – logically – the greater the chances of a more dangerous strain emerging …

But rest assured: no virus becomes so deadly that it wipes out its host population. Quite simply because that would mean destroying its own resources, ecosystem and environment – destroying itself, in other words. I may not be intelligent, but I'm not so stupid that I'd destroy my own environment. Who would be that crazy?

Why the clitoris doesn't get the attention it deserves – and why this matters

Jane Chalmers
Lecturer in Physiotherapy, Western Sydney University

Cat Jones
Artist in Residence, Body In Mind, Sansom Institute, University of South Australia

10 March 2016

Did you know the clitoris is a large and complex organ? If not, it's probably not your fault: in anatomical textbooks, few words and diagrams are devoted to understanding the clitoris. Most label the very small portion of the organ visible on diagrams of the vulva, when in fact it's almost entirely under the skin.

Studies of historical anatomical textbooks have shown that depictions of the clitoris were significantly limited and often omitted completely from the mid-19th into the 20th century (see, for example, 'Clitoral conventions and transgressions: Graphic representations in anatomy texts' by Lisa Jean Moore and Adele Clarke).

During these times there were ideologies and subsequent theories relating to women's bodies that likely encouraged and sustained censorship of the clitoris. For instance, there was Freud's now defunct theory that clitoral stimulation was a sign of sexual immaturity and neurosis. Women were also taught not to enjoy sex; women had sex for reproductive purposes, while men had sex for pleasure.

These fallacies led to the neglect of the clitoris in research, literature and the public domain.

Although more recent research (see, for example, the 'Cliteracy' project in the *Huffington Post*) and feminist lobbying have improved the quality of information on the clitoris in current textbooks, most texts are still brief. These include minimal information, or information only on the external portion of the clitoris (the glans). This brevity has impacts on health care for women with clitoral and related pain.

What is the clitoris?

The clitoris lies at the junction of the labia minora (the inner lips of the vulva), just above the urethra. It is made up of four main parts: the glans, body, two crura and two bulbs. The glans is the only external part of the clitoris and is covered by a hood of skin.

The body, corpora, crura and bulbs of the clitoris are all made up of erectile tissue and converge below the glans. The body of the clitoris is generally 1–2 centimetres wide and 2–4 centimetres long.

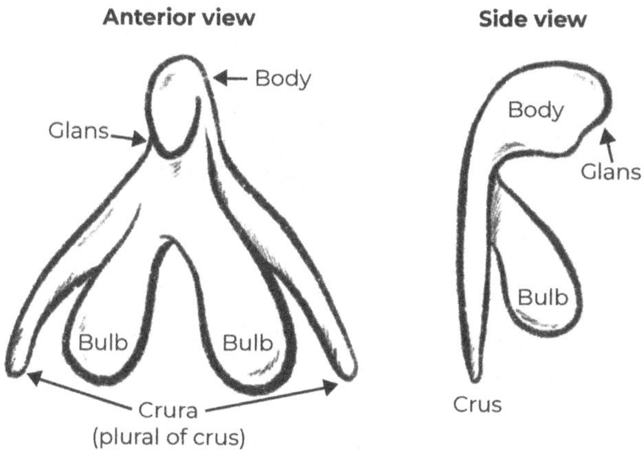

Left: the clitoris from an anterior view. All four parts of the clitoris are visible in this view: the glans (external portion), the body, the bulbs and the crura. Right: the clitoris from a side view. Only one crus (plural: crura) and bulb are shown from this view. Note, the clitoris is a tri-planar organ, with each component lying in a different plane to one another. (Image: Wes Mountain)

The crura extend laterally from the body of the clitoris and are on average around 5–9 centimetres long. The bulbs of the clitoris are generally 3–7 centimetres long and lie between the body, crura and the urethra.

The clitoris is highly innervated, with twice as many nerve endings as the penis, and receives a rich blood supply. This rich blood supply allows the erectile components to swell up, with the body and glans of the clitoris becoming up to three times larger during arousal – and you thought a penile erection was impressive!

Foetus genital and reproductive organs are differentiated at six weeks' gestation. While the clitoris and penis arise from the same group of cells in a zygote, we now know they clearly have different forms and functions.

The penis has an obvious and well-researched role in the reproductive and urinary systems, while the function of the clitoris is usually stated as being purely for pleasure.

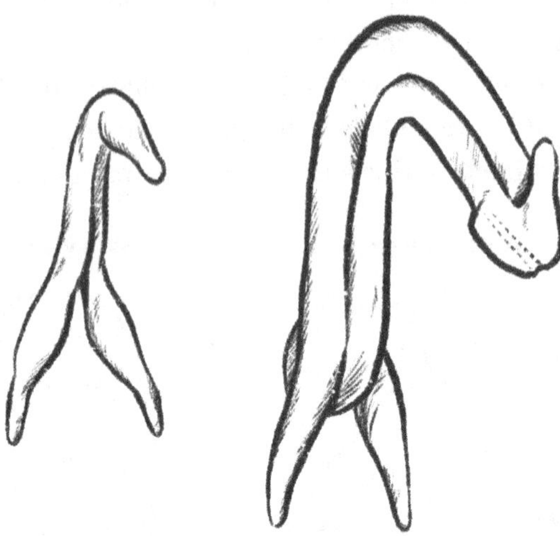

The clitoris (left) and penis (right) emerge from the same cells in a zygote. (Image: Wes Mountain)

However, few studies have actually investigated the function of the clitoris. The close proximity of the clitoris to the urethra and vagina has led to suggestions it plays a much larger role than sexual pleasure, such as assisting in maintaining immune health.

What we don't know can hurt us

Censoring the clitoris in textbooks means doctors and other health-care professionals won't be equipped to treat patients with clitoral concerns. Women are at risk of sexual dysfunction (such as lack of desire or arousal, decreased lubrication, inability to orgasm) from operations on their urinary and reproductive organs. This shows doctors need more in-depth knowledge, and we need further research into understanding the anatomy of the clitoris.

Because of its delicate yet complex make-up, the clitoris is prone to infections, inflammation and diseases. Some common examples are itching and soreness due to thrush infections, swelling due to bruising or inflammation, and pain of unknown origin (called clitorodynia).

Although it is not often spoken about, clitoral and vulvar pain are very common in women.

Educating patients about their condition can improve pain outcomes. Yet, this may be difficult for doctors treating conditions such as clitorodynia, given they may not be receiving adequate information about the clitoris themselves.

On average, one-third of university-aged women are unable to find the clitoris on a diagram. We frequently use synonyms for females' reproductive organs as derogatory terms ('pussy' to mean weak, 'cunt' to mean an unpleasant person) and many women are often not comfortable using anatomically correct terms.

More than 65 per cent of women say they feel uneasy using the terms vagina and vulva. Instead they use code names such as 'lady parts', even when discussing gynaecological issues with their doctors.

Given there is evidence to suggest our sense of body ownership can influence pain (see, for example, 'Bodily illusions in health and disease: Physiological and clinical perspectives and the concept of a cortical "body matrix"' by G Lorimer Moseley et al.), perhaps this lack of body ownership over the clitoris helps to explain why conditions such as clitorodynia are common.

What causes autism? What we know, don't know and suspect

Andrew Whitehouse
Bennett Chair of Autism, Telethon Kids Institute, University of Western Australia

19 February 2016

One of the great and enduring mysteries of autism is what causes the brain to develop so differently. The behavioural differences of many individuals with autism are so apparent that it seems intuitive the causes would also be obvious.

But research over the past seventy years has indicated this isn't so. Into this knowledge gap have come all sorts of weird and wacky ideas about the causes of autism: television, power lines, vaccines and sex position during conception. None have any credence but have fuelled the mystery surrounding what may cause autism.

In the 1950s and 1960s, there was a widely held belief autism was caused by parental coldness towards the child. The term 'refrigerator mother' was often directed at the mothers of these children.

Leo Kanner, the man who first described the behaviours that characterise autism, explored 'a genuine lack of maternal warmth' as a possible explanation for autism. This inaccurate belief left a legacy of shame and guilt in the autism community for at least the following two decades.

Several eminent scientists, such as Bernard Rimland, eventually extinguished the myth. Two of them were themselves parents of children with autism, and they highlighted a major flaw in the theory: parents who fitted the 'refrigerator' stereotype also had children who did not have autism.

Since this time, research has focused on biological factors that may lead to autistic behaviours. This has found, very clearly, there is no one cause of autism.

A variety of genetic factors are likely to be the ultimate cause of most cases of autism. These may work by themselves, or in combination with environmental factors, to lead a child's brain to develop differently and result in autistic behaviours.

Genetics

To examine the influences of nature (genetics) and nurture (environment) on a given human quality, scientists study twins.

To appreciate how these studies work, it's first important to understand there are two types of twins. Identical twins share all of their DNA and, assuming they grow up in the same household, they will also share all of their environment. Fraternal twins also share all of their environment, but only around half of their DNA, just like non-twin siblings.

Twin studies start by defining a clear population – say, the metropolitan area of a city – and finding in that area as many sets of twins as possible where one or both of the twins have the given trait of interest – in this case, autism.

Scientists then look at the 'concordance' of that trait – that is, the percentage chance that if one twin has autism, the other twin will also have autism. If the concordance is higher for identical twins than fraternal twins, then we can say the difference is due to the increased amount of genetic material shared by the identical twins, and that autism is influenced by genetics.

The first twin study of autism was conducted in 1977 on eleven identical and ten fraternal twins across Great Britain, where at least one of the twins had autism (see 'Infantile autism: A genetic study of 21 twin pairs' by Susan Folstein and Michael Rutter). Concordance for identical twins was 36 per cent, compared with 0 per cent for the fraternal twins.

While the study was only small in size, it provided the first evidence that autism may be genetic in origin. Since this pioneering study, more than a dozen further twin studies have confirmed this original observation.

The best current estimate is that there is a 50–80 per cent concordance for identical twins and a 5–20 per cent concordance for fraternal twins. This indicates a strong genetic component to the condition. The figure for fraternal twins – 5–20 per cent – also represents the chance of a couple who already have a child with autism having a second child with autism (referred to as the 'recurrence risk').

Once scientists have established that the cause of a disorder is influenced by genes, the next task is to identify the exact genes that might be involved. However, after several decades of intensive research, scientists could find no one genetic mutation that all individuals diagnosed with autism shared.

It was these findings (or lack of findings) that led scientists to stop thinking of autism as one condition with one cause. They started viewing it as many different conditions, which all have relatively similar behavioural symptoms.

This new view of autism has proved extremely fruitful in discovering subtypes of autism. For example, a number of conditions have very clear genetic or chromosomal abnormalities that can lead to autistic behaviours.

These include disorders that have abnormalities of the chromosomes, such as Down syndrome. While no chromosomal condition itself accounts for any more than 1 per cent of individuals with autism, when combined they account for approximately 10–15 per cent of all individuals diagnosed with autism.

The exact genetic abnormalities that may lead to the remaining cases of autism are not completely clear. There are two reasons for this.

The first is that the genetic regions involved are likely to be very complex. Scientists have needed to develop new techniques to examine them.

The second is that it is probable the genetic mutations are very rare and complex. The DNA chain that forms our chromosomes contains more than 3 billion building blocks. To identify small pieces of DNA that may be linked to the development of autism among so many base pairs, scientists need to study a very large number of people with autism.

To date, no study has been able to examine the thousands of people necessary to identify with accuracy all of the small mutations that might lead to autism.

However, with genetic technologies improving at an astronomical pace, as well as global scientific cooperation that will lead to large numbers of people being studied, major advances in the understanding of the causes of autism are probable in the very near future.

A likely prospect is that many cases of autism will be related to what is called 'common genetic variation'. This refers to differences in genes that are also found in many individuals who do not have autism and by themselves are not sufficient to lead to autism. However, when multiple genetic risk factors are found in the same person, they combine to have a major effect on how the brain develops.

A small proportion of autism cases are also likely to be caused by what are known as *de novo* ('new') mutations. Most often, the egg and sperm that create a baby contain genetic material that is present in the mother and father, respectively. However, in rare cases, the egg and sperm may contain genetic material that is not found in either parent. There is now good evidence that some people with autism may have inherited *de novo* genetic mutations that have an effect on brain development.

Environmental causes

Recognition has grown over the past decade that aspects of our environment may also contribute to autism. However, despite substantial research, no one environmental factor has yet been found to be a definite cause of autism.

The most widely used research technique to examine environmental risk factors for autism is epidemiology, which examines how often, and why, diseases occur in different groups of people.

Several environmental factors during prenatal life have been linked with autism. Bacterial or viral infections in the mother during pregnancy have been found to slightly increase the risk of autism in the offspring. This could be due to the passage of harmful infectious organisms from the mother to the foetus through the placenta, or because the immune response of the mother may be detrimental to the developing brain of the foetus.

Other factors in the mother that may be related to offspring autism include a folic acid deficiency at the time of conception, the presence of gestational diabetes and the use of certain antidepressants during pregnancy, but no conclusive evidence exists for any of these links.

Being an older parent, particularly an older father, is also thought to increase the risk of having a child with autism. As males get older, the number of sperm that contain *de novo* genetic mutations increases.

Some of the *de novo* genetic mutations will have minimal or no effect on the resulting baby, but some mutations can lead to the brain developing differently.

Several studies have found that fathers who are over fifty at the time of conception have a greater chance of passing on *de novo* mutations and also a greater risk of having a child with autism.

An obvious, but very important, observation is that not all people who are exposed to these factors are diagnosed with autism. One possible explanation for this is a phenomenon called gene–environment interaction, which is when the genetic make-up of two different people leads them to respond differently to an environmental factor.

Brain development

For a considerable time, scientists were searching for one clear brain difference that may lead to autistic behaviours. However, this hope has yet to be fulfilled, with few studies identifying brain characteristics that are shared by different individuals diagnosed with autism.

This may be a further indication that autism has many different causes, but it may also be a reflection of the difficulties in studying the brain.

Currently, scientists use a variety of clever techniques to understand the structure and function of the brain, such as magnetic fields, X-rays and radioactive chemicals. As ingenious as these methods are, they are unable to provide a full measure of the tremendous complexity of how the brain operates.

It is also unlikely that autism affects just one area of the brain. The complex behaviours of individuals with autism, which include cognitive, language and sensory difficulties, make it hard to pinpoint just one brain region that may be affected. Nevertheless, some promising leads have shown how different brain pathways may lead to autistic behaviours.

There is increasing evidence that differences in brain development may begin prenatally in some individuals with autism. Several studies of prenatal ultrasound measurements have found evidence for differences in the growth patterns of the brain in foetuses later diagnosed with autism. Newborns later diagnosed with autism are often also reported to have large heads at birth (macrocephaly).

Another research technique has been to dissect the brains of individuals with autism who have prematurely died, so-called post-mortem studies. A recent study that examined the brains of eleven autistic individuals at the microscopic level found changes in the structure and organisation of the brain cells that form during foetal life, indicating differences in brain development that begin very soon after conception. (See 'Patches of disorganization in the neocortex of children with autism' by Rich Stoner et al.)

Another well-studied area in autism is head circumference growth in the first years of life. This research dates back to 1943 and Leo Kanner's original study that found five of the eleven children with autism he examined had large heads.

Several small studies throughout the 1990s and 2000s searched the medical records of relatively small groups of children with autism. These found that a key period was the first two years of life, in which a minority of children later diagnosed with autism had a marked increase in the rate of growth of their head.

During the first two years of life, the size of an infant's head is a reasonable indicator of total brain size, and for many years 'brain overgrowth' during very early development was seen as a risk factor for a later diagnosis of autism.

However, more recently, this view has been challenged by the release of the largest-ever study in this area, which found no link between infant head circumference growth and autism. (See 'Early head growth in infants at risk of autism' by Lonnie Zwaigenbaum et al.)

Studies using brain imaging machines have examined whether parts of the brains of individuals with autism may be different in size, shape or function.

However, the only consistent finding is just how much inconsistency there is. Not every individual with autism has differences in the size or pattern of growth of different brain regions. For those individuals who do, it is unclear how this may relate to their autistic behaviours.

A great deal of brain imaging research has examined the connections within the brain of individuals with autism. Connectivity is a measure of how well and how much two brain areas communicate with each other. In the study of autism, scientists distinguish between short-range connections (between neighbouring brain areas) and long-range connections (between brain areas further apart).

One prominent theory that has emerged from brain imaging studies is that some individuals with autism may have under-connectivity in long-range connections, but over-connectivity in short-range connections.

If found to be accurate, these brain differences may be able to explain why some individuals with autism have difficulties with complex tasks that require the integration of information from multiple brain regions (such as cognitive and social abilities), but have no difficulties, or even enhanced abilities, with tasks that require less integration across brain areas (such as sensory processing).

Other biological factors

There is preliminary evidence some but not all individuals with autism are exposed to higher levels of testosterone in the womb. Excessively high testosterone concentrations in the bloodstream can be harmful and cause cells to die, particularly within the brain, which is highly sensitive to changes in hormone levels.

One thought is that the pattern of cell death caused by high testosterone levels may alter brain development in a way that leads to autistic behaviours in childhood. This theory is still to be proven. Again, it is certain that not all individuals with autism are exposed to excessive levels of testosterone in the womb.

The link between gastrointestinal ('gut') problems and autism is another scientific area that has received a great deal of attention. It is now well known that between 30 and 50 per cent of individuals with autism experience significant gastrointestinal problems, such as diarrhoea, constipation and an irritable bowel.

It has long been a mystery why, but there is now extremely good evidence that the complex community of microbes in the gut plays an important role in human development and is essential for healthy immune and endocrine systems, as well as the brain.

Some scientists believe a disruption in the natural balance of these 'good' bacteria may be a potential cause of autism. Antibiotics, for example, are commonly used on infants in Western societies and are known to kill 'good bacteria' along with the 'bad' bacteria for which they were prescribed.

A difference in the community of microbes, which humans have evolved to rely upon, may disrupt brain development and lead to autism. At the present time, the evidence for this potential cause of autism is not strong, but there will be substantial research in this area in coming years.

Autism has no one single cause, both in terms of genes and the brain. In a minority of cases, there are very clear genetic abnormalities that cause autism. In other cases, the genetic differences are more complex and yet to be discovered.

While there is currently no evidence for any environmental causes, it is possible subtle influences of the environment may affect individuals differently depending on their genetic make-up, leading to autism in some children. These relationships are also yet to be discovered.

Psychopaths versus sociopaths: What is the difference?

Xanthe Mallett
Senior Lecturer in Forensic Criminology, University of New England

28 July 2015

'Psychopath' and 'sociopath' are popular psychology terms to describe violent monsters born of our worst nightmares. Think Hannibal Lecter in *The Silence of the Lambs* (1991), Norman Bates in *Psycho* (1960) and Annie Wilkes in *Misery* (1990). In making these characters famous, popular culture has also burnt the words used to describe them into our collective consciousness.

Most of us, fortunately, will never meet a Hannibal Lecter, but psychopaths and sociopaths certainly do exist. And they hide among us. Sometimes as the most successful people in society because they're often ruthless, callous and superficially charming, while having little or no regard for the feelings or needs of others.

These are known as 'successful' psychopaths, as they have a tendency to perform premeditated crimes with calculated risk. Or they may manipulate someone else into breaking the law, while keeping themselves safely at a distance. They're master manipulators of other peoples' feelings but are unable to experience emotions themselves.

Sound like someone you know? Well, heads up. You do know one; at least one. Prevalence rates come in somewhere between 0.2 and 3.3 per cent of the population.

If you're worried about yourself, there are many online quizzes so you can check, but before you click on that link, let me save you some time: you're not a psychopath or sociopath. If you were, you probably wouldn't be interested in taking that personality test.

You just wouldn't be that self-aware or concerned about your character flaws. That's why both psychopathy and sociopathy are known as antisocial personality disorders, which are long-term mental health conditions.

What's the difference?

Psychopaths and sociopaths share a number of characteristics, including a lack of remorse or empathy for others, a lack of guilt or ability to take responsibility for their actions, a disregard for laws or social conventions, and an inclination to violence. A core feature of both is a deceitful and manipulative nature. But how can we tell them apart?

Sociopaths are normally less emotionally stable and highly impulsive – their behaviour tends to be more erratic than psychopaths'. When committing crimes – either violent or non-violent – sociopaths will act more on compulsion. And they will lack patience, giving in much more easily to impulsiveness and lacking detailed planning.

Psychopaths, on the other hand, will plan their crimes down to the smallest detail, taking calculated risks to avoid detection. The smart ones will leave few clues that may lead to being caught. Psychopaths don't get carried away in the moment and make fewer mistakes as a result.

Both act on a continuum of behaviours, and many psychologists still debate whether the two should be differentiated at all. But for those who do differentiate between the two, one thing is largely agreed upon: psychiatrists use the term psychopathy to illustrate that the cause of the antisocial personality disorder is hereditary. Sociopathy describes behaviours that are the result of a brain injury, or abuse and/or neglect in childhood.

Psychopaths are born and sociopaths are made. In essence, their difference reflects the nature versus nurture debate.

There's a particularly interesting link between serial killers and psychopaths or sociopaths – although, of course, not all psychopaths and sociopaths become serial killers. And not all serial killers are psychopaths or sociopaths.

But America's Federal Bureau of Investigation (FBI) has noted certain traits shared between known serial killers and these antisocial personality disorders. These include predatory behaviour (for instance, Ivan Milat, who hunted and murdered his seven victims); sensation-seeking (think hedonistic killers who murder for excitement or arousal, such as twenty-one-year-old Thomas Hemming, who, in 2014, murdered two people just to know what it felt like to kill); lack of remorse; impulsivity; and the need for control or power over others (such as Dennis Rader, an American serial killer who murdered ten people between 1974 and 1991, and became known as the 'BTK (bind, torture, kill) killer').

A case study

The Sydney murder of Morgan Huxley by twenty-two-year-old Jack Kelsall, who arguably shows all the hallmarks of a psychopath, highlights the differences between psychopaths and sociopaths.

In 2013, Kelsall followed Huxley home, where he indecently assaulted the thirty-one-year-old before stabbing him twenty-eight times. Kelsall showed no remorse for his crime, which was extremely violent and premeditated.

There's no doubt in my mind he's psychopathic rather than sociopathic because, although the murder was frenzied, Kelsall showed patience and planning. He had followed potential victims before and had shared fantasies he had about murdering a stranger with a knife with his psychiatrist a year before he killed Huxley, allegedly for 'the thrill of it'.

Whatever Kelsall's motive, regardless of whether his dysfunction was born or made, the case stands as an example of the worst possible outcome of an antisocial personality disorder: senseless violence perpetrated against a random victim for self-gratification. Throughout his trial and sentencing, Kelsall showed no sign of remorse, no guilt, and gave no apology.

A textbook psychopath, he would, I believe, have gone on to kill again. In my opinion – and that of the police who arrested him – Kelsall was a serial killer in the making.

In the end, does the distinction between a psychopath and sociopath matter? They can both be dangerous and even deadly, the worst wreaking havoc with people's lives. Or they can spend their life among people who are none the wiser for it.

Health Check: The science of 'hangry', or why some people get grumpy when they're hungry

Amanda Salis
NHMRC Senior Research Fellow in the Boden Institute of Obesity, Nutrition, Exercise & Eating Disorders, University of Sydney

20 July 2015

Have you ever snapped angrily at someone when you were hungry? Or has someone snapped angrily at *you* when *they* were hungry? If so, you've experienced 'hangry' (an amalgam of hungry and angry) – the phenomenon whereby some people get grumpy and short-tempered when they're overdue for a feed.

But where does hanger come from? And why is it that only some people seem to get hangry? The answer lies in some of the processes that happen inside your body when it needs food.

The physiology of hanger

The carbohydrates, proteins and fats in everything you eat are digested into simple sugars (such as glucose), amino acids and free fatty acids. These nutrients pass into your bloodstream from where they are distributed to your organs and tissues and used for energy.

As time passes after your last meal, the amount of these nutrients circulating in your bloodstream starts to drop. If your blood-glucose levels fall far enough, your brain will perceive it as a life-threatening situation. You see, unlike most other organs and tissues in your body, which can use a variety of nutrients to keep functioning, your brain is critically dependent on glucose to do its job.

You've probably already noticed this dependence your brain has on glucose; simple things can become difficult when you're hungry and your blood glucose levels drop. You may find it hard to concentrate, for instance, or you may make silly mistakes. Or you might have noticed that your words become muddled or slurred.

Another thing that can become more difficult when you're hungry is behaving within socially acceptable norms, such as not snapping at people. While you may be able to conjure up enough brain power to avoid being grumpy with important colleagues, you may let your guard down and inadvertently snap at the people you are most relaxed with or care most about, such as partners and friends. Sound familiar?

Another bodily response

Besides a drop in blood-glucose concentrations, another reason people can become hangry is the glucose counter-regulatory response. Let me explain.

When blood-glucose levels drop to a certain threshold, your brain sends instructions to several organs in your body to synthesise and release hormones that increase the amount of glucose in your bloodstream.

The four main glucose counter-regulatory hormones are: growth hormone from the pituitary gland situated deep in the brain; glucagon from the pancreas; and adrenaline, which is sometimes called epinephrine, and cortisol, which are both from the adrenal glands. These latter two glucose counter-regulatory hormones are stress hormones that are released into your bloodstream in all sorts of stressful situations, not just when you experience the physical stress of low blood-glucose levels.

In fact, adrenaline is one of the major hormones released into your bloodstream with the 'fight or flight' response to a sudden scare, such as when you see, hear or even think about something that threatens your safety. Just as you might easily shout out in anger at someone during the 'fight or flight' response, the flood of adrenaline you get during the glucose counter-regulatory response can promote a similar reaction.

Nature and nurture

Another reason hunger is linked to anger is that both are controlled by common genes. The product of one such gene is neuropeptide Y, a natural brain chemical released into the brain when you are hungry. It stimulates voracious feeding behaviours by acting on a variety of receptors in the brain, including one called the Y1 receptor.

Besides acting in the brain to control hunger, neuropeptide Y and the Y1 receptor also regulate anger or aggression. In keeping with this, people with high levels of neuropeptide Y in their cerebrospinal fluid also tend to show high levels of impulse aggression.

As you can see, there are several pathways that can make you prone to anger when you're hungry. Hanger is undoubtedly a survival mechanism that has served humans and other animals well. Think about it like this: if hungry organisms stood back and graciously let others eat before them, their species could die out.

While many physical factors contribute to hanger, psychosocial factors also have a role. Culture influences whether you express verbal aggression directly or indirectly, for instance.

And as we are all different across all of these factors, it's little wonder there are differences in how angry people seem to get when they're hungry.

Dealing with hanger

The easiest way to handle hanger is to eat something before you get too hungry. While you may hanker for quick-fix foods, such as chocolate and potato chips, when you're in the throes of hanger, junk foods generally induce large rises in blood-glucose levels that come crashing down fast.

Ultimately, they may leave you feeling hangrier. So think nutrient-rich, natural foods that help satisfy hunger for as long as possible, without excess kilojoules.

Eating as soon as you are hungry may not always be possible. This may be the case during long shifts at work, for instance, or through religious fasts such as Ramadan, or during weight-loss diets that involve severe energy restriction (such as intermittent fasting diets). These should only be done if your doctor has given you the all-clear.

In these cases, it can help to remember that, with time, your glucose counter-regulatory response will kick in and your blood-glucose levels will stabilise. Also, when you go without food, your body starts breaking down its own fat stores for energy, some of which are converted by your body into ketones, a product of fat metabolism. Ketones are thought to help keep your hunger under control because your brain can use ketones in place of glucose for fuel.

A final – and very civilised – way of handling hanger is that difficult situations be dealt with *after* food, not before!

PART V

A new philosophy

No, you're not entitled to your opinion

Patrick Stokes
Senior Lecturer in Philosophy, Deakin University

5 October 2012

Every year, I try to do at least two things with my students at least once. First, I make a point of addressing them as 'philosophers' – a bit cheesy, but hopefully it encourages active learning.

Second, I say something like this: 'I'm sure you've heard the expression "Everyone is entitled to their opinion." Perhaps you've even said it yourself, maybe to head off an argument or bring one to a close. Well, as soon as you walk into this room, it's no longer true. You are not entitled to your opinion. You are only entitled to what you can argue for.'

A bit harsh? Perhaps, but philosophy teachers owe it to our students to teach them how to construct and defend an argument – and to recognise when a belief has become indefensible.

The problem with 'I'm entitled to my opinion' is that, all too often, it's used to shelter beliefs that should have been abandoned. It becomes shorthand for 'I can say or think whatever I like' – and by extension, continuing to argue is somehow disrespectful. And this attitude feeds, I suggest, into the false equivalence between experts and non-experts that is an increasingly pernicious feature of our public discourse.

First, what's an opinion?

Plato distinguished between opinion or common belief (doxa) and certain knowledge, and that's still a workable distinction today: unlike '1+1=2' or 'there are no square circles', an opinion has a degree of subjectivity and uncertainty to it. But 'opinion' ranges from tastes or preferences, through views about questions that concern most people, such as prudence or politics, to views grounded in technical expertise, such as legal or scientific opinions.

You can't really argue about the first kind of opinion. I'd be silly to insist that you're wrong to think strawberry ice cream is better than chocolate ice cream. The problem is that sometimes we implicitly seem to take opinions of the second and even the third sort to be unarguable in the way questions of taste are. Perhaps that's one reason (no doubt there are others) why enthusiastic amateurs think they're entitled to disagree with climate scientists and immunologists and have their views 'respected'.

Meryl Dorey is the leader of the Australian Vaccination Network, which, despite the name, is vehemently anti-vaccine. Ms Dorey has no medical qualifications but argues that if former Greens leader Bob Brown is allowed to comment on nuclear power despite not being a scientist, she should be allowed to comment on vaccines. But no one assumes Dr Brown is an authority on the physics of nuclear fission; his job is to comment on the policy responses to the science, not the science itself.

So what does it mean to be 'entitled' to an opinion?

If 'Everyone's entitled to their opinion' just means no one has the right to stop people thinking and saying whatever they want, then the statement is true, but fairly trivial. No one can stop you saying that vaccines cause autism, no matter how many times that claim has been disproven.

But if 'entitled to an opinion' means 'entitled to have your views treated as serious candidates for the truth', then it's pretty clearly false. And this too is a distinction that tends to get blurred.

On Monday, the ABC's *Media Watch* program took WIN-TV Wollongong to task for running a story on a measles outbreak, which included comment from – you guessed it – Meryl Dorey. In a response to a viewer complaint, WIN said the story was 'accurate, fair and balanced and presented the views of the medical practitioners and of the choice groups'. But this implies an equal right to be heard on a matter in which only one of the two parties has the relevant expertise. Again, if this was about policy responses to science, this would be reasonable. But the so-called 'debate' here is about the science itself, and the 'choice groups' simply don't have a claim on airtime if that's where the disagreement is supposed to lie.

Media Watch host Jonathan Holmes was considerably more blunt: 'there's evidence, and there's bulldust', and it's not part of a reporter's job to give bulldust equal time with serious expertise.

The response from anti-vaccination voices was predictable. On the *Media Watch* site, Ms Dorey accused the ABC of 'openly calling for censorship of a scientific debate'. This response confuses not having your views taken seriously with not being allowed to hold or express those views at all – or to borrow a phrase from the writer Andrew Brown, it 'confuses losing an argument with losing the right to argue'. Again, two senses of 'entitlement' to an opinion are being conflated here.

Next time you hear someone declare they're entitled to their opinion, ask them why they think that. Chances are, if nothing else, you'll end up having a more enjoyable conversation that way.

This is why you will lose your argument

Peter Ellerton
Lecturer in Critical Thinking, University of Queensland

15 June 2015

So, the Great Barrier Reef has not been listed as endangered by UNESCO. And same-sex marriage is high on the national agenda. Care to argue the case for or against? Careful, there's a minefield ahead.

There is one thing that is poorly understood about arguing in the public arena. It is why a strong case will often lose its momentum and that an obvious, logical conclusion will be missed. It is one of the reasons our political leaders fail utterly to have a rational conversation with the population and with each other. And it's why denialists on just about any issue can sidestep rational debate.

It's called the 'point at issue' and describes what the argument is *actually* about. If you move away from this simple idea, the argument will be lost in a fog of related but unnecessary issues.

Finding the point

Before we can argue, we must actually agree on something: what we are arguing about. If we can't do this, and then stick to it, there will be no progress.

Let's consider the Great Barrier Reef as an example. Some media commentary would have us believe that the fact the reef was not listed means any concerns about its wellbeing are entirely misplaced.

This misses the point completely. As many articles have pointed out, that the reef has not been listed does not mean any environmental concerns are unjustified.

The point at issue is whether the reef meets the UNESCO criteria for listing as endangered. It is another point entirely to say the reef is not at risk. Conflating the two muddies the waters.

As another example, imagine someone comments that locking up refugees is psychologically damaging to them. Another person says that the policy is much better under the current government than it was under the last.

The argument has shifted from whether the process is damaging to who manages the process best. It is not the same thing. If that is not noticed, the argument usually degenerates and we are no closer to finding the truth of the original claim.

For a third example, the Federal Treasurer, Joe Hockey, recently had to defend spending his accommodation entitlements when he is in Canberra, on a house owned by his wife. He tried to argue the necessity of politicians to be able to claim expenses as they move into the capital for parliamentary business. But these are two different points. Arguing the second does not progress the first.

Deniers of climate science engage in shifting the point at issue as a standard part of their argument technique. One example involves moving from the fact that there is a rapid shift in global temperature to climate having always changed.

Another example is moving from consilience and consensus in climate science as indicators of the degree of confidence within the scientific community, to trying to make the debate that consensus is not proof. In both cases the latter point is true, but it's not the point under discussion.

Changing the point at issue often flags an attempt to move the argument onto more favourable ground rather than engage with it on the offered terms.

Focusing our thinking is not easy

This type of intellectual sidestepping is the root of the straw man argument. It is the source of the common phrase 'beside the point', indicating it is not directly relevant.

If we follow this path, the original argument remains unaddressed and we have only the illusion of progress.

The trick is to recognise when the point at issue shifts, but to do this you need to be very clear at the start about what the original argument is.

If you are not clear, you are vulnerable to defeat, losing to an argument that was not your point in the first place. Recognising this shift is a surprisingly difficult thing to do.

One of the reasons we do not focus well on the point at issue, and are sometimes very bad at defining it, is that our minds range across related topics very well. We see connections, implications and perspectives on many issues. This is a useful tendency, but one that needs to be curbed to develop a sharp argumentative focus.

If the point at issue is that smoking is bad for you, don't start talking about the individual liberty to smoke. If it's that biodiversity in forests is important, don't make it about logging jobs. If it's about how well a political party is doing a job, don't turn it into a comparison with the other mob.

Stick to the point, sort it out properly, and then move on to the next one.

How we frame an issue can define the argument

Finding the point at issue is also a matter of framing the issue correctly.

Realise, for example, that the point of not teaching intelligent design in science classes is one of quality control, not of academic freedom. Or that teaching about religion in schools is not the same thing as instruction in specific religions. Or that same-sex marriage is about equality of rights, not degrading them.

As the journalist Christopher Hitchens so succinctly put it when considering the issue of homosexual marriage more than a decade ago: 'This is an argument about the socialisation of homosexuality, not the homosexualisation of society.'

Politicians are masters at changing frames and the point at issue. Witness the use of phrases like 'what the public really wants to know' or 'what's really important here' to avoid addressing the issue raised in an interview.

Journalists are often very lax about this, allowing the point at issue to change without bringing it back and pressing for an answer to the original question.

One of the skills of advanced argumentation – and of good journalism – is knowing how to keep things on track. This includes the ability to recognise when the argument shifts and to say 'that's not what we are talking about'.

It also includes knowing how to go on and explain to people that their argument may be relevant to the topic in general but it's not relevant to the specific point at issue.

You might like to argue that many of the topics I've mentioned should be explored in full. That we should talk about biodiversity and jobs when discussing forests, for example. But if you think that, you missed the point at issue of this article.

There's no reason not to pursue other arguments and other points at issue, but let's take them one at a time for the sake of clarity and improvement. This is what will benefit public debate and better hold politicians to account.

That's what I'm talking about.

Twelve ways to deal with a climate change denier – the BBQ guide

Will J Grant
Researcher / Lecturer, Australian National Centre for the Public Awareness of Science, Australian National University

Rod Lamberts
Deputy Director, Australian National Centre for Public Awareness of Science, Australian National University

22 December 2014

The end of the year is nigh and it's a time for Christmas and New Year parties and gatherings. In the Southern Hemisphere that means barbecues and beaches. In the Northern Hemisphere it's mulled wine and cosy fireplaces.

But for all of us, it probably means we'll be subjected to at least one ranting, fact-free sermon by a Typical Climate Change Denier (TCCD).

You know the drill. Make an offhand remark about unusual weather, and five seconds later someone's mouthing off about how the internet says climate change is a bunch of rubbish.

So, when you've been cornered by your TCCD, what do you do?

As many have said before, disagreements like this aren't resolved by barrages of facts and figures. But that doesn't mean you just have to walk away.

Instead of providing you with yet another series of climate facts and figures (there are plenty of excellent examples of these already, such as the website *Skeptical Science*), we've listed twelve tips, strategies and tactics for you to try out when you next feel inclined to engage a TCCD head-on.

Good luck! And remember – it's a party, so, you know, have fun with it.

1. Pick your audience

Most TCCDs will not change their mind. It's cheaper – intellectually and socially – for them to stand their ground than it is to change their views. Actually, your arguing may even reinforce their beliefs.

But remember – you might convince their friends listening in.

2. Find some common ground

Just because your TCCD thinks they know better than pretty much all of science doesn't mean they're a bad person. They value things and are probably well-intentioned at heart.

So, try finding out what they care about: democracy or economics, knitting or veggie gardening. You may even have some shared interests. You'll never get them to change their values, but you might be able to talk about climate change in terms of things they care about.

3. Certainty isn't the issue

Your TCCD may say we don't understand climate change with 100 per cent certainty, so we shouldn't do anything. They're right about the first point, but utterly wrong about the second.

Climate science isn't 100 per cent certain, but neither is medicine, the law, child-rearing or pretty much anything else. We make decisions without certainty every day.

Complete certainty is pretty much never required for action.

4. Talk in terms of risk and inaction

Ask them this: 'What's worse, the majority of climate change scientists being wrong but we act anyway, or climate change deniers being wrong and we don't?'

Challenge them to be specific, to go beyond vague assertions of terribleness or repeating empty tabloid slogans.

5. Compare the risk to something more tangible

Do they trust doctors? Try saying: 'So, have you ever taken a doctor's advice, like if they recommended you lose some weight or get that weird growth biopsied?'

Doctors rarely guarantee that bad things will happen if you ignore their advice, but it's pretty damned risky to gamble that they won't.

6. Speaking of doctors and second opinions

It's not just one opinion here. Research says 97 per cent of climate doctors believe the planet has a bad case of human-induced climate change, and the prognosis isn't great (see 'Debunking 97% climate consensus denial', *Skeptical Science*).

While there is likely to be some wiggle room in the exact percentage, it's fair to say consensus is very high.

And if ninety-seven (or even nine) doctors told you that you had life-threatening but treatable cancer, would you act? Or would you keep looking until you found one doctor who told you not to worry about it, that the cancer isn't serious, and that it's all just a medical conspiracy to sell you chemotherapy?

7. The TCCD with an inkling of scientific knowledge

This trickster knows not all scientific discoveries were immediately accepted by mainstream science. Plate tectonics and the Earth orbiting the sun leap to mind.

While scientific mavericks are few and far between, they do exist. But simply being a maverick doesn't make anyone right. Most of the time it just makes them wrong.

8. Wait for them to say, 'It's all a big conspiracy'

Sigh. There are those who claim climate change is the lab-coat version of the John F Kennedy assassination or the moon landing 'hoax'.

Really?

The idea of an international conspiracy across dozens of disciplines, hundreds of institutions and thousands of individuals is honestly laughable. If the world's climate scientists were so good at conspiracy, they'd be better off using their astounding Machiavellian skills to rig an election or clean up on the stock market.

Also, anyone who actually uncovered such a scam would win all of the Nobel prizes at once.

9. Climate scientists are in it for the money

Have you seen the pay scale of a typical research scientist in Australia? Tell the TCCD to go to any university car park and count the luxury vehicles parked near science buildings. They won't even need all their fingers to keep track.

A related gem is the line that Al Gore and co. are doing this because they invested in renewable energy companies and want to make money.

Okay, what makes more financial sense?

1. Create a bogus scare requiring a global conspiracy of academics and scientists and grand appeals for huge amounts of controversial and untested R&D in countries all over the world *and then* wait for that to gain traction in financial markets and eventually drag in wads of cash.
2. Invest money in existing, lucrative and proved enterprises today and cash in right now.

10. Why pick on climate science?

The odds are they will happily accept – even applaud – any science that isn't climate change related.

Ask them if they accept gravity, nutrition, internal combustion engines or maths? If they say 'yes', probe them on why climate science is different. If they say 'no', back away slowly.

Interestingly, TCCDs often endorse mitigation options that support business-as-usual use of fossil fuels, even while asserting human-induced climate change isn't happening. That's a fun little 'gotcha' if you're in the mood.

11. Scientists don't actually want it to be true

Challenge them to find a single, legitimate source that shows a bona fide climate change scientist who is happy about what they are finding and what their findings mean.

We've been working around such folks for years and have not even heard of one. Seriously, not one.

12. CO_2 isn't a pollutant

This is another claim touted by TCCDs – that CO_2 itself isn't inherently poisonous. It's important for plants, so therefore it can't be bad.

Their underlying logic is that you can never have too much of a good thing – ask them if they realise that's what they're arguing, then give them your best scornful school teacher stare.

Too much of anything can be dangerous, hence the phrase 'too much'. You can even be killed by drinking too much water.

Now, get back to the BBQ

Anyone who's challenged a TCCD knows that trying to turn them is usually frustrating and annoying. They are rarely part of the solution and probably never will be.

But that doesn't mean challenging them is always futile.

You can sometimes encounter someone who's genuinely interested in ground-truthing their position (yes, it does happen). You could also be inspiring nearby partygoers to think more – or differently – about the climate situation.

In the end, every little bit counts. If you have even a small influence in a positive direction, that's not a bad thing to come out of Christmas drinks. At worst, at least you have an opportunity to hone your debating (and trolling) skills.

Cheers and good luck!

A sports car and a glitter ball are now in space – what does that say about us as humans?

Alice Gorman
Associate Professor in Archaeology and Space Studies, Flinders University

7 February 2018

Two controversial objects have recently been launched in space, and their messages couldn't be more different.

One is Elon Musk's red sports car, a symbol of elite wealth and masculinity, hurtling towards Mars.

The other is a glittering geodesic sphere in Earth's orbit, designed to give humans a shared experience and a sense of our place in the universe: the Humanity Star.

A red car for a red planet

On 6 February 2018, Musk's private space company, SpaceX, launched the much-vaunted Falcon Heavy rocket from Kennedy Space Center – from the same launch pad as Apollo 11 in 1969.

It's a test launch carrying a dummy payload: Musk's own personal midnight cherry Roadster, a sports car made by his Tesla company. The driver, dubbed Starman, is a mannequin in a SpaceX spacesuit.

For the ultimate road trip soundtrack, the car is playing David Bowie's 'Space Oddity'.

The car will enter an elliptical solar orbit, its furthest point from the sun around the distance of Mars.

Musk thinks of it as future space archaeology.

Reactions include waxing lyrical about the speed the car will reach, lamenting the lost opportunity for a scientific experiment, and celebrating it as an inspirational act of whimsy (see 'Elon Musk's Roadster will break the record for fastest a car has ever traveled' by Jay Bennett).

Fear of flying

The Tesla Roadster might be an expendable dummy payload, but its primary purpose is symbolic communication. There's a lot going on here.

There's an element of performing excessive wealth by wasting it. Giving up such an expensive car (a new model costs US$200,000) could be seen as a sacrifice for space, but it's also like burning $100 notes to show how little they mean.

In the 1960s, anthropologist Victor Turner argued that symbols can encompass two contradictory meanings at the same time. Thus, the sports car in orbit symbolises both life and death. Through the body of the car, Musk is immortalised in the vacuum of space. The car is also an armour against dying, a talisman that quells a profound fear of mortality.

The spacesuit is also about death. It's the essence of the uncanny: the human simulacrum, something familiar that causes uneasiness, or even a sense of horror. The Starman was never alive, but now he's haunting space.

In a similar vein, the red sports car symbolises masculinity – power, wealth and speed – but also how fragile masculinity is. Stereotypically, the red sports car is the accessory of choice in the male midlife crisis, which men use to rebel against perceived domestication.

A related cultural meme holds that owning a sports car is overcompensation. Have we just sent the equivalent of a dick pic into space?

Space graffiti

The brainchild of Peter Beck (founder of the New Zealand-based Rocket Lab), the Humanity Star was launched on 21 January 2018, but kept a secret until after it had successfully reached orbit.

In contrast to the lean and slightly aggressive lines of the sports car, the Humanity Star is a geodesic sphere of silver triangular panels. It's a beach ball, a moon, a BB-8, a space age sculpture. Its round shape is friendly and reassuring.

Similar satellites – with reflective surfaces designed for bouncing lasers – are orbiting Earth right now. But this satellite doesn't have a scientific purpose. Its only function is to be seen from Earth as its bright faces tumble to catch the light.

Astronomers weren't happy, saying that it would confuse astronomical observations. It was even called 'space graffiti', implying its visual qualities marred the 'natural' night sky. Some lambasted Rocket Lab for contributing to the orbital debris problem. Instead of inspiration, they saw pollution.

Through the looking glass

Beck wants people to engage with the Humanity Star. In his words,

> My hope is that everyone looking up at the Humanity Star will look past it to the expanse of the universe, feel a connection to our place in it and think a little differently about their lives, actions and what is important.
>
> Wait for when the Humanity Star is overhead and take your loved ones outside to look up and reflect. You may just feel a connection to the more than seven billion other people on this planet we share this ride with.

This is the 'Overview Effect' in reverse. We can't all go to space and see the whole blue marble of the Earth from outside, inspiring a new consciousness of how much we are all together in the same boat. Beck has tried to create a similar feeling of a united Earth by looking outwards instead.

In nine months or so, the Humanity Star will tumble back into the atmosphere to be consumed. It will leave no trace of its passage through orbit.

The medium is the message

Ultimately, these orbiting objects are messages about human relationships with space. Both objects were launched by private corporations, inviting Earthbound people to share the journey. However, one reinforces existing inequalities, while the other promotes a hopeful vision of unity.

Beck's and Musk's intentions are irrelevant to how the symbols are interpreted by diverse audiences. Symbols can be multivalent, contradictory and fluid – their meanings can change over time, and in different social contexts.

Every object humans have launched into the solar system is a statement: each tells the story of our attitudes to space at a particular point in time.

Curious Kids: Does space go on forever?

Tanya Hill
Honorary Fellow of the University of Melbourne and Senior Curator (Astronomy), Museums Victoria

26 April 2017

Curious Kids is a series aimed at children. Send your child's question to curiouskids@theconversation.edu.au *and our editors will find the perfect expert to answer their query. There's no such thing as a silly question!*

Does space go on forever? – Conrad, age 6, Sydney

Space probably does go on forever, but the truth is we don't know. Not yet, anyway. That's what makes this a great question, because science is all about finding answers to things we don't know yet.

So, what do we know about space? We know it's big, really big. It's big enough to contain the Earth and all the other planets. It's big enough to include the sun and all the stars we see at night.

Not that long ago, people thought that when they looked up at the night sky, they were seeing all of space. That was until Edwin Hubble came along. He was an American astronomer and what he found out was so amazing that NASA named the Hubble Space Telescope after him.

Stars far, far away

Almost 100 years ago, Hubble, the astronomer, was looking at some small, fuzzy patches of light hidden among all the stars we can see. No one was exactly sure what they were, but Hubble discovered that these patches of light were made of stars and, even more importantly, they were a long way away.

With that one discovery, our idea of space exploded.

The stars we see in the night sky are part of the Milky Way Galaxy. That's the galaxy we belong to.

The patches of light that Hubble was studying were other galaxies – each one filled with stars and planets and lots of other things too. Some galaxies are smaller than our Milky Way and others are larger.

Space was a whole lot bigger than anyone had ever imagined.

How to see forever?

Space is big, but does it go on forever? The problem is, we can't see forever. There's a limit to how much space we can see, just like we can't step outside our front door and see every city in Australia.

The part of space we can see is called the observable universe. It contains all the light we will ever be able to see (because when we look across space we are mostly looking for light).

The observable universe can even be measured. It is 93 billion light years from one side to the other.

Now, that's a distance even astronomers find hard to think about. It's like making about 300,000 laps of our Milky Way Galaxy, yet our sun has made only 20 laps in its entire life. Or can you imagine lapping the Earth 20 million trillion times?

What's more, the observable universe is centred on us because we are at the centre, looking out into space. An alien on another planet, in a faraway galaxy, would have their own observable universe. You might want to think of each of us being inside our own bubble universe.

If our two bubbles overlapped, then the alien would see some of the same things we can see. But what about the places that are outside our bubble? Would the alien see emptiness at the edge of space?

No, probably not. What's more likely is they would see a part of space that we will never ever be able to see.

In theory, space goes on and on ...

Why do scientists think that space goes on forever? It's because of the shape of space. Our part of space, or the observable universe, has a special shape: it is flat.

That means if you and a friend each had your own rocket ship sitting side by side on a launch pad, and you both took off straight up into space, as long as each of you continued travelling in a straight line, forever and ever, you would never meet. In fact, you would always stay exactly the same distance apart, within the observable universe.

But this is a really special case. If space was shaped any other way, then lots of things could happen. Your two rockets, travelling in a straight line, might eventually cross paths, or they might get really close but never meet, or perhaps they'd go in the other direction and drift away from each other.

But only flat space will keep the rockets exactly apart.

Scientists have an idea of how to solve this special flatness problem. And, importantly, their idea solves some other problems as well, to explain why space looks exactly the way we see it.

When one idea solves lots of problems, scientists call it a theory. It means we could be on the right track to finding an answer.

The theory says that space must be really, really big but we can only see a small part of it, and that part looks special and flat. It's kind of like how Earth seems flat, unless you are an astronaut floating in space. Up there, you see so much more of the Earth that it's possible to see how it curves away.

My bet is that space does go on forever. Maybe one day science will help tell us if that's true.

PART VI

The decade in politics

Why is the Confederate flag so offensive?

Clare Corbould
Associate Professor, Deakin University

24 July 2020

Most Australians – aside from a few groups dedicated to re-enacting American Civil War battles and history buffs including Bob Carr and Kim Beazley – were not familiar until recently with the charged history of the flag of the Confederate States of America.

Now the flag is in the Australian news, with reports SAS military in Afghanistan in 2012 used the bold red, blue and white flag to guide in a US helicopter. Two SAS personnel also posed for a photograph with the flag.

Why do these images of Australian soldiers posing with a flag from another country's long-ago war provoke such strong reactions? Because the flag has long symbolised defiance, rebellion, an ideal of whiteness, and the social and political exclusion of non-white people – in a word, racism.

The Confederacy defeated, but not punished

The flag represents the Confederate States of America (CSA or Confederacy), created in 1861, when eleven states seceded from the eighty-five-year-old nation. This rebellion was prompted by the election of Abraham Lincoln as President. Lincoln argued slavery should not be extended to new territories the United States was annexing in the west. Southern enslavers feared slavery in their established states would be Lincoln's next target.

The ensuing four-year Civil War between the CSA and US was resolved in 1865, with the defeat of the Confederacy and the near-abolition of enslavement.

In the aftermath of the war, a longer battle began: how to interpret the war. For 155 years, this struggle has turned largely on the contradiction that although the US fought to end slavery, most white Americans, including in the north, had little commitment to ending racism.

After a decade of military occupation of the south, known as the period of Reconstruction, the US military withdrew its forces. White southerners, who had retained their land, implemented unjust legal and labour systems, underpinned by violence and racist ideas about Black people's inferiority.

Memorials of war

The re-embrace of white southerners into the nation showed a desire to 'heal' the nation by downplaying the horrors of enslavement and the struggle to end it.

New narratives depicted the war as a righteous, though tragic, struggle over 'states' rights'. By avoiding a conversation as to what those rights were about – that is, enslavement – by the 1890s, they remade the meaning of the war.

Confederate flags were a powerful symbol in reinterpreting the War of the Rebellion. In the 1915 box-office hit feature film *The Birth of a Nation*, for example, the central battle scene involves a key character, Ben Cameron of South Carolina, ramming the pole of a Confederate flag down a United States army cannon.

In the very next shot, however, the injured Cameron is rescued from the no-man's land between trenches by his long-time family friend, northerner and US Army commander Phil Stoneman.

The movie's second half cemented the theme of reconciling white southerners and white northerners. As it stated in an intertitle, 'The former enemies of North and South are united again in common defense of their Aryan birthright'. It even became a tool to recruit new members to the Ku Klux Klan.

The war, in this telling, was a struggle between white and Black Americans, not between the US and the rebel Confederacy.

Blowing in the wind

The Confederate flag featured prominently in *Gone with the Wind* (1939), another immensely popular film that again glorified the way of life of white southerners during and immediately after slavery. In this case, however, Hollywood used the more visually striking Confederate battle flag, which General Robert E Lee had flown during the war, rather than any of the CSA's national flags.

As the heroine, Scarlett O'Hara (Vivien Leigh), arrives at a makeshift hospital, the camera pans back to a field of hundreds of wounded and dead soldiers. The scene shifts only once those soldiers are framed by a Confederate flag, blowing majestically in the breeze.

These two films buttressed a political economy that relied on a cheap labour force of disenfranchised Black Americans. But as African-Americans began to make headway in the fight for civil rights, starting during World War II, symbols such as the Confederate flag became even more important to those who felt affronted by their gains.

Enter the 'Dixiecrats'

In the late 1940s, a new political party of southerners opposed President Harry S Truman and the Democratic Party's relatively sympathetic stance on civil rights.

These 'Dixiecrats' adopted the Confederate battle flag as their party's emblem. From that point, the flag was clearly associated with racist opposition to civil rights and with umbrage at perceived government intrusion into the lives of individuals.

When civil rights activism was at its most visible, in the 1950s and 1960s, many white southerners became firmly attached to the flag.

The state of Georgia, where resistance to desegregation was fierce, adopted a new state flag that incorporated the Confederate flag.

A few years later, in 1961, neighbouring state South Carolina began flying the Confederate flag above its state Capitol.

Banning the flag

In 2000, after years of protest, South Carolina legislators moved the Confederate flag to the State House's grounds. Then, after white supremacist Dylann Roof endorsed the Confederate flag and murdered nine Black churchgoers in 2015, activist Bree Newsome shimmied up the pole and removed it in a galvanising act of civil disobedience.

Two weeks later, the flag in South Carolina's house of government was finally removed for good. In the years since, hundreds of Confederate flags, statues and memorials have disappeared, including in the national Capitol.

In 2016, recognising the flag's toxic history, major retailers announced they would no longer sell the flag.

In the wake of George Floyd's murder, the removal of Confederate symbols has accelerated. In recent months, southern company Nascar has banned the flag and the Department of Defense has effectively done so too.

In a polarised political and media environment, many white southerners continue to defend their allegiance to the Confederate flag.

They claim the battle flag represents their southern heritage, as if that heritage comprises an innocent history of mint juleps and church-going. The problem with that claim, as the history of the use of the flag demonstrates, is that the heritage it symbolises is also that of enslavement, inequality, violence and gross injustice.

Courting the chameleon: How the US election reveals Rupert Murdoch's political colours

Denis Muller
Senior Research Fellow, Centre for Advancing Journalism, University of Melbourne

16 November 2020

Joe Biden's victory in the US presidential election raises a perennial question about what Rupert Murdoch does when the candidate he has opposed wins.

Answer: he adapts and he waits. Electoral cycles last three, four or five years. Murdoch has been wielding power for five decades.

Murdoch is a chameleon. It is true that when political and business conditions are favourable he glows brightly in blood-red conservatism. But when, as now, conditions are uncertain, the colour dims and takes on a more complex hue.

The voices and front pages of the empire become more diverse. It gets harder to exactly pin down where the emperor himself stands. He deflects awkward questions by saying he defers to his editors, or he claims to have retired and says he will speak to the heir, his son Lachlan.

These are the first steps in a shadowy repositioning, and we have seen it happen time without number.

Reactionary ideology is important to Murdoch, but not as important as making money.

Money not only keeps the shareholders happy, it provides the means by which he can subsidise his unprofitable or barely profitable newspapers because they are crucial to the way he wields power.

So, the priority when a disfavoured candidate or party wins is to do nothing to antagonise the new regime and instead proffer a small olive branch. Last Sunday's *New York Post* banner headline – 'It's Joe Time' – was a classic of the genre.

Over on Fox News, he remained quiet when the Fox 'decision desk' called the crucial state of Arizona for Biden, absorbing pressure and entreaties from Trump's people to intervene.

All of a sudden, the chorus of pro-Trump voices on Fox became a discordant racket. Some, like Sean Hannity, amplified Trump's claims of electoral fraud. Others, like Neil Cavuto, cut off Trump's press secretary for making the same claims.

The *New York Post*, which ran a highly questionable story against Hunter Biden in the last week of the campaign, was suddenly dismissing Trump's claims as baseless and urging him to accept the result.

Conflict, confusion and contradiction are part of the strategy. Murdoch allows it to unfold. It sends a signal to the Biden White House: we can live with you.

The strategy was helped along on 13 November, when Trump sent out a tweet saying the daytime ratings on Fox News had collapsed because they had forgotten what made them successful: the 'Golden Goose' – an immortal self-description if ever there was one.

There was a similar pattern to the Murdoch strategy in Australia in 2007, when it looked certain that Labor under Kevin Rudd would end the long reign of John Howard.

In his book *Rupert Murdoch: A Reassessment*, Rodney Tiffen recounted that, while Murdoch did not want to be backing the losing side, it was difficult for his editors to persuade him to back Rudd.

In the end, some of Murdoch's papers, including *The Australian*, backed Rudd, while others, including Melbourne's *Herald Sun*, were allowed to back the Coalition.

The endorsements were pallid, nothing like the full-throated propaganda characteristic of the Murdoch papers when they are unified behind a conservative cause. The chameleon had turned into a blur of pale reds and blues.

Then in 2018, when it looked as if Labor might beat Malcolm Turnbull's Coalition in 2019, Murdoch once again showed how the business pragmatist triumphs over the ideologue.

According to Turnbull, in his autobiography, *A Bigger Picture*, Murdoch told the West Australian media mogul Kerry Stokes: 'Three years of Labor wouldn't be too bad.'

He prefers it when the Labor side is led by moderates who are amenable to business: Bob Hawke, Paul Keating, Britain's Tony Blair. But, even then, his endorsements tend to be muted, nothing like 'Kick this mob out' on the front page of Sydney's *Daily Telegraph* when he opposed Labor in 2013.

In Britain, Murdoch has employed the same tactics. Although his mass-circulation *The Sun* supported Labour in 1997, 2001 and 2005, he allowed the prestigious *Sunday Times* to support the Conservatives.

But when it comes to endorsing the conservative side of politics, there is no pussyfooting around.

When he turned on Labour after Gordon Brown had succeeded Blair as Prime Minister, he unleashed the full Murdoch treatment.

Just as Brown was about to deliver his speech to Labour's annual conference in September 2009, *The Sun* declared Murdoch's abandonment of Labour with the banner headline 'Labour's lost it'.

From then until the 2010 election, Murdoch's ruthless campaign in support of David Cameron's Conservative Party was carried by all his papers, *The Sun* in the vanguard, with headlines such as 'Brown toast'.

At elections, Murdoch has two priorities.

One is always to try to ensure the new regime, whatever its political colour, does not implement regulatory change that will disadvantage the business.

The second is to be on the winning side. This is important to the maintenance of the belief – at least in the minds of politicians – that he is a kingmaker.

When it is clear the progressive side of politics is in the ascendant, the chameleon can start changing colours early and might even complete a transformation before election day.

When it is not a sure thing, however, the skin-deep transformation has to begin when the results come in.

That is what is on display in the US now.

Donald Trump's America: A cloud cuckoo land devoid of fact, evidence and argument

Raimond Gaita
Professorial Fellow, Faculty of Arts and the Melbourne Law School, University of Melbourne

15 November 2016

Many people in America and elsewhere are scared of what Donald Trump will do. As I write, some are in the street protesting that he is not 'their President'. Many of the same people are also bewildered, still incredulous that he became even the Republican candidate, let alone the President-elect.

Never has a candidate in a Western democracy shown such contempt for the conventions upon which democratic accountability depends. Never has a politician seeking office insulted and threatened so many of his fellow citizens. Trump is praised for giving voice to the justifiable anger of a 'forgotten' white working class, but in doing it, he encouraged contempt – even hatred – of many of their fellow citizens, and reckless disregard of the kind of man he is and what he said he would do.

Commentators now describe him as an unconventional politician who ran an unconventional campaign. Is it merely unconventional to threaten to ban Muslim immigration? To lament the fact you cannot any more just take hecklers at a rally aside and 'beat the shit out of them'? To express pleasure at the prospect of torturing suspected terrorists in ways 'far worse' than waterboarding them? To lead crowds in the chant 'lock her up', when the person they are referring to is your opponent in the race for the presidency? To display such contempt for women that most prominent Republicans disowned him?

One could go on. To call him unconventional, or even radically unconventional, is to forget how important are the conventions, often unspoken, that enable decency in politics. He has poured a can of excrement over those conventions.

Trump also did something that, while it might seem less dramatic, is perhaps more dangerous. His demagoguery took political discourse in America to a place where it lost contact with reality. We normally think of demagoguery as a threat to reasonable discussion because it whips up fear, resentment, hatred and prejudice to such a pitch that it throws reason into a ditch.

But demagoguery can displace reason – or, as I prefer to put it, the conditions of sober critical judgement – more radically and more dangerously though it is not overthrown by emotion and prejudice. Trump did that. I shall try to explain why I say that.

The end of reason

We know politicians sometimes lie. Indeed, we know that political life would be impossible were that not so. But I do not remember anyone in mainstream democratic politics who lied so shamelessly, so often and so fast, that the fact-checkers could not keep up with him.

Trump's disdain of facts and argument became so persistent and extreme that he took his supporters – and America with them – into a place where he eroded the conditions that enable the application of concepts of fact, evidence and argument. Or, more precisely, to where argument can make, or fail to make, evidence out of facts. His demagoguery took from reason, not the calm necessary for its operation, but the concepts necessary for its application.

English writer GK Chesterton said: 'A madman is not the man who has lost his reason. The madman is the man who has lost everything except his reason.'

He said this in a polemic on behalf of imagination against reason, about which I have reservations. But his point can be put more generally like this: the proper functioning of reason depends on being in contact with reality, but it cannot secure that contact.

Think of a paranoid. His ingenuity in marshalling arguments, and his responses to claims that the evidence will not support his suspicions and fears, are parodies of reason. Confronted with such a person, we realise that the concept of irrationality cannot capture what has gone wrong. It's not just too weak; it's in the wrong dimension. We reach naturally for the idea that he is out of touch with reality, and that reason cannot prevent anyone from being taken there or lead anyone back to reality.

Was Trump at least sometimes mad? Did he take his supporters to the edge of madness? My argument does not require that we conclude that. There are many ways of losing touch with reality – believing that the Earth is flat, or even considering it a serious possibility, or believing that Elvis is alive and working for the FBI, for example. But that his demagoguery had the effect not only of humiliating reason in the face of extreme emotion and prejudice, but also of taking people into cloud cuckoo land, is, I believe, partly the reason why he won the election. It helps explain the distinctive nature of the bewilderment about the fact that he did.

If someone like Ted Cruz, who placed second behind Trump in the Republican primary, or someone with more charisma than Cruz, had won on the same policies, then people in America and around the world would also be frightened. Many Americans would also be protesting that he is not their President. But they would not be incredulous in the way they now are because they do not know where they are or how they got there.

In an attempt to explain that incredulity and also why pollsters got the results wrong, observers have said the media and, indeed, the political establishment on both sides took Trump literally but did not take him seriously, whereas those who secured his victory did not take him literally but took him seriously.

But what can it mean to take someone seriously when he has taken you into cloud cuckoo land, when he lies so often and shamelessly and when he is so often inconsistent and doesn't care that he is? The distinction these observers draw depend on one's living in a conceptual, conversational, space in which the concept of sober judgement has not been eroded.

Cloud cuckoo land – out-of-touch-with-reality-land – is not such a space. To believe that someone is serious while believing that to be a virtue is to assume that they are sufficiently integrated as one person over time. That they have integrity in this literal sense – to be accountable, to be answerable to a call to seriousness: 'Can you really mean this! How could you say that? How can I trust you when you lie again and again. For God's sake, *think*!' And so on.

The trouble, as I said before, is not just that Trump wouldn't listen or that he would duck and weave. That would merely make the call to seriousness unlikely to succeed, rather than to erode the conceptual space in which it is possible to make it.

The conditions of accountability eroded

It is one thing to be defeated by people with whom one strongly disagrees. It is another to be defeated by someone who eroded the conditions of accountability. Then it seems that one is reduced to babbling. Or shouting. Or screaming. Or, perhaps forced to violence. People are calling for wounds inflicted during the campaign to be healed. There can be no healing until there is a sober reckoning with that fact and what it implies.

Democracy as we know it depends on an ideal that one could always, in principle, call one's fellow citizens to seriousness if they voted for polices that one found unjust, or demeaning or that simply affected one's interests badly. In modern times it shows in the way we engage one another on talkback radio. But to call someone to seriousness assumes they can rise to it, that unless they are children they do not need more education to do it. It is not controversial that hostility to what are generally called 'elites' is widespread among Trump supporters. It showed also in Brexit, and now shows in Europe, where quasi-fascist parties have taken heart from Trump's victory. It shows here, in Australia, though its political consequences are far less dangerous.

To be very poor is one thing. To be unjustly forced into poverty is worse. To be forgotten is worse still. But to be looked down upon, to be treated with disdain, can inflame a rage so fierce that it cares nothing for the consequences of its expression. Trump's opponent, Hillary Clinton, said that half of Trump's supporters were 'deplorables'.

She apologised, but those who felt they were her targets did not believe she meant it. Many of the people who voted for Trump were referred to as 'non-college educated'. Who could resist the inference that the deplorables were also the non-college educated and that really they were, simply, uneducated.

Political theorist Hannah Arendt said that one should never engage with one's fellow citizens as though they are in need of education. That would be arrogant, smug and incipiently authoritarian. University education does not of itself make one wise, or even very critically minded. If it did, there would not be such uniformity of opinion among its beneficiaries.

Nor does it of itself develop in its beneficiaries a concern for truth over the many vices – vanity, the need for approval, cowardice, careerism – that subvert a serious pursuit of it, the kind of pursuit that people like the philosopher John Stuart Mill hoped would lead to a more enlightened politics. From the perspective of the uneducated, the deplorables, it is more likely to make you 'politically correct'. Or one of the chattering classes, in the derogatory sense of that expression. Those expressions are weapons in the culture wars.

I do not want to discuss those wars here. In their aggressive, mean-spirited refusal to grant that behind the sometimes foolish expression of an opponent's opinion, there is something serious to consider, often supported by a tradition of some depth, they poison everything they touch. But there can be no doubt that Trump won the culture wars, or, at any rate, a very important battle in them, decisively, as the Brexiters did before him.

Which is not to deny that the education systems here and in America failed to teach the elementary aspects of good argument – of being conscientiously attentive to relevant, factual evidence and of thinking logically, being patiently careful about how to move from one thought to another.

Developing a capacity to think critically

But the capacity to think critically requires also that we develop an ear for tone, for what rings false, for what is sentimental, or has yielded to pathos and so on. The development of such a sensibility is not optional in reflection about the human condition; indeed, about anything that matters ethically. Without it we are easy prey for demagogues, especially in turbulent times such as we now live in.

Education in the more basic forms of argument and the sensibility whose character I have just sketched should begin at primary school. This education should be conducted in such a way that someone who does not go on to university can never for that reason be suspected of being in need of further education in order to be fully respected as a fellow citizen, possessing all that he needs to be deserving of that respect.

Australia is not likely to produce a demagogue like Trump. We are, as someone said recently on *Q&A*, a 'better society'. But in Australia, disillusionment with politicians is deep and turning to cynicism. Australians vacillate between disillusionment and cynicism.

The difference between cynicism and disillusionment is important. Disillusionment is informed by standards, holds politics to account to those standards, but reckons it has failed to be accountable to them.

Cynicism has given up on the standards as even applicable to politics. At its worst, it mocks and even despises them.

To such people, the expressions 'the dignity of politics', or 'morality and politics' are oxymorons. The sources of our disillusionment and cynicism are many, but one, I think, is our justified belief that politicians constantly insult our intelligence. Thankfully, if my ear for this is right, dismay about this crosses cultural, educational and economic boundaries. This is one reason why Australia will not find its Trump.

Some years ago, when I returned to Australia after living in London under Tony Blair's government, it struck me that though Australians tended to be cynical about certain aspects of politics, they believed they had the measure of their politicians. They expected them to lie, and provided that the lies did not seriously affect their material interests, they were not too bothered by this form of mendacity.

They felt they had their feet firmly planted on the ground. By contrast, it seemed to me that after being subjected for many years to very sophisticated spin, Britons could no longer locate the ground in order to plant their feet on it.

Spin is a form of mendacity more dangerous to politics than lying, unless the lying takes on Trump-like proportions. That will not happen in Australia. But spin can have a similar effect, as Britons realised. It does not, of itself, make one lose touch with reality, but it can make contact with reality less secure.

A few weeks after September 11, 2001, together with a specialist in Greek Philosophy, MM McCabe, I conducted a seminar on Plato's dialogue, *Gorgias*, at King's College London. In that dialogue, Socrates announces his affirmation that it is better to suffer evil than to do it. It has haunted Western thought about the relations between morality and politics.

The atmosphere in that seminar was electrifying. Everyone knew what was at stake in that affirmation. Recommendations that we should make torture lawful were already making ground. The dialogue begins with an attack on oratory (read spin). Orators, Socrates says, lose touch with reality and with themselves. Oratory (again, read spin) could never be neutral means to be used for good or ill: it is rotten through and through.

How astonishing, but also wonderful, that a little book written over two and a half thousand years ago could teach us so much today.

Capital against country, young against old: Brexit Britain is broken Britain

Sean Lang
Senior Lecturer in History, Anglia Ruskin University

25 June 2016

Is Brexit Britain Prime Minister David Cameron's famous 'broken Britain'? The bitterness of the referendum campaign and the divides it has revealed within the Conservative Party and between the Labour Party and its core supporters certainly suggest so.

Deep rifts now run between old and young, London and England, England and Scotland. The prospect of a second referendum on Scottish independence is now firmly in play.

The Remain camp argued for a Britain playing its full part in Europe and accused Brexit of wanting a 'little England'. Is that what we have all woken up to this morning?

'Little Englander' is a rather contemptuous term originally used by Victorian supporters of the Empire. It was used especially with reference to Britain's role in the Boer War to denigrate their opponents and critics, who they accused of wanting to keep Britain small and ineffectual in a world of global European empires.

More recently it has been used by pro-Europeans to accuse Brexiters of much the same thing in a world of regional unions. Are they right? Has the electorate's decision to back Brexit revealed Britain as a little country, a small island, inward-looking and parochial?

It depends first on what we mean by Britain. Modern little Englanderism hardly applies in Scotland. England and Wales may have turned their backs on Europe but Scotland, true to its continental links dating back to the Declaration of Arbroath (1320) emphatically did not. The fear of Scottish independence made not a jot of difference to voting intentions in England or Wales on Thursday. Did English and Welsh voters realise they were clearly turning their backs on Edinburgh as well as on Brussels? Maybe, but they didn't care. Perhaps they hate the EU even more than they value the Union.

Prime Minister Benjamin Disraeli spoke of England as 'two nations' – the rich and the poor. Modern England is just as divided but along a different fault line. This referendum was a revolt of the provinces against the domination of the capital. Not since London rallied to the side of parliament and drove out Charles I have capital and country been so much at odds.

For all the talk of immigration – and this was par excellence a vote about immigration – there is a certain irony that the most immigrant-rich part of the whole country voted overwhelmingly to remain.

Young people, unhindered by memories of World War II or the immediate post-war period, are much more European in outlook than the older generation, who voted for a nostalgic 'golden age' when, they assume, Britain was Great.

The Brexit campaign's 'take back control' slogan was a canny exercise in nostalgia politics. It suggested there was a time before 1973 when Britain was fully in control of its destiny. But was there? Britain had twice sought entry to the European Economic Community before 1973 precisely because it felt so economically and politically powerless in its post-imperial role. Is it now about to return to that state of impotence?

Two years after the Conservative Prime Minister Edward Heath took Britain into the European Economic Community he was himself thrown out of office in a general election fought on the question 'Who Rules Britain?' David Cameron has now been brought down by a referendum fought on much the same question. As we survey the ravaged political landscape that has resulted, the question must now be: what sort of Britain has Brexit left his successor to govern?

Why Australia Day survives, despite revealing a nation's rifts and wounds

Frank Bongiorno
Professor of History, ANU College of Arts and Social Sciences, Australian National University

22 January 2018

Wendy McCarthy checked anxiously for signs of rain when she went to bed the night before Australia Day in 1988. A senior manager with the Australian Bicentennial Authority, McCarthy was staying at a hotel in The Rocks, Sydney, so she could wake up close to the action the following day.

McCarthy rose early to what sounded like rain. Fearing the worst, she rushed to the window. But the sound that had alarmed her was not rain. It was thousands of Australian feet, shuffling in their sneakers and thongs, to the biggest party the country had ever seen. 'It was my moment to weep with relief,' she reflected in her memoir. 'Everyone had decided to be there.'

Not quite everyone, perhaps, but Sydney Harbour was soon teeming with activity; of spectator craft, but also of tall ships and First Fleet re-enactment vessels, one of them famously bearing a Coca-Cola logo on its sails. Crowds lined the shores – some slept overnight in caves to get a nice possie – and millions more watched on television around the nation.

While Australia Day is an occasion for barbecues, concerts and fireworks, as well as the display of flags that no one has any use for at other times, it has never been as spectacular since.

As a public holiday, it marks the boundary between the summer break – even for those who have long since returned to work – and the rest of the year.

For students, it announces the return to the world of uniforms, teachers, classes and books. For most of us, the normal balance (or imbalance) of work and leisure asserts its authority, even as we still swelter in blistering heat.

Australia Day is, among other things, a seasonal festival, like May Day is to the northern spring. Many, perhaps most, Australians are no more likely to reflect deeply on its historical significance than maypole dancers are inclined to ponder phallic symbolism. Some would have difficulty naming the historical event that Australia Day commemorates, the arrival of the First Fleet in 1788. If pressed, they might tell you it was when Captain Cook turned up at Botany Bay.

It has long had its critics. In 1938, the year of the sesquicentenary of settlement, the Aborigines Progressive Association declared it a Day of Mourning and Protest. In the lead-up to the Bicentenary, Aboriginal activists embraced the slogan 'White Australia Has a Black History'. They said 26 January 1788 was a day of invasion.

On the day of the Bicentenary in 1988, thousands of Indigenous people who had come from all over the country, as well as white sympathisers and supporters, marched through Sydney in protest. Some set up with flags and banners at Mrs Macquarie's Chair near Sydney Harbour. Later, many would head out to Kurnell, near Botany Bay, the site of Cook's arrival in 1770, for a night of traditional dancing, followed in the morning by a smoking ceremony.

So, what has changed with Change the Date? Social media have provided new opportunities for such campaigns. But the change since the 1980s is profound.

What was still just a counter-narrative in 1988 – one only partly absorbed into the historical consciousness of settler Australians – now more thoroughly permeates their sense of the Australian story. Those were times before the *Mabo* High Court decision, before the reconciliation movement and before the ascendancy of the Stolen Generations narrative.

Today, even if they are hazy about detail, white Australians increasingly appreciate that 26 January is for many Indigenous people a day of sadness, reminding them of dispossession, violence and suffering.

Some disagree, claiming to speak for ordinary Australians unimpressed with the latest iteration of political correctness. Former Labor Party leader turned right-wing activist Mark Latham tells us: 'It's a day of national unity and celebration where people can feel genuinely proud of being Australian.'

Yet, that he felt the need to tell us so, while launching an advertising campaign in partnership with Indigenous leader Jacinta Price to save Australia Day, only serves to highlight the contentious and increasingly divisive nature of the day.

Last year, responding to a couple of Melbourne councils announcing they would not conduct citizenship ceremonies on the day, the conservative historian Geoffrey Blainey also condemned 'the latest move against Australia Day', which was 'often led by suburban Greens'. Blainey declared: 'At a time when there is a widespread fear that the nation could be weakened by the hidden circles of Muslim terrorists, more social cohesion is essential.'

It may be doubted whether Australia Day can do much to protect us from such a menace. To be sure, here and abroad, the state has long used national days to promote national unity. Australia Day was celebrated as

Anniversary Day in Sydney in the early decades of white settlement, with an annual dinner, and sporting events such as boat and horse races.

But in the late 19th century, a Victorian-based organisation of white native-born men, the Australian Natives' Association (ANA), campaigned in favour of 26 January becoming a public holiday and the national day. It was sometimes subsequently known as ANA Day.

National days proliferated around the world, as nation-states invented traditions aimed at mobilising their populations in the years leading up to World War I. One historian, Eugen Weber, famously called this the process of turning 'peasants into Frenchmen'.

But the idea that 26 January might become Australia's national day developed only slowly, not least because from 1916 it was competing to some extent with Anzac Day. The various civic rituals and occasions that now grace Australia Day – such as citizenship ceremonies and the announcement of the Australian of the Year awards and the honours list – were progressively grafted on to the day from the mid-20th century onwards. The historian Ken Inglis, writing in 1967, reported that Australia Day was not marked in any public manner in Canberra at that time.

The problem for those who have harboured grand ambitions for Australia Day is that it is not our answer to Independence Day in the United States or to Bastille Day in France. Australia had no revolution.

The break that Australia Day marks is not that between dependence and independence, colony and republic, or the despotism of the old order versus the liberty, equality and fraternity of the new – even if strident Australia Day advocates do wax lyrical about the gift to Indigenous people of Western civilisation that the British arrival in 1788 so generously bestowed.

Australia Day will likely survive because of its seasonality. As a summer public holiday supporting some modest civic activity and public spectacle, it retains the backing (and money) of government and of a still considerable and powerful section of civil society. And it remains a popular occasion for social gatherings.

But as it becomes ever more entangled in battles over the meaning of our history, Australia Day will find it difficult to carry a 'successful' national day's normal civic burden of fostering common belonging and social cohesion.

The Morrison government's biggest economic problem? Climate change denial

Judith Brett
Emeritus Professor of Politics, La Trobe University

19 October 2018

Last week, former Federal Treasurer Peter Costello accused former Prime Minister Malcolm Turnbull of failing to develop an economic narrative to unite the Coalition. Turnbull promised this when he challenged Tony Abbott for the leadership of the Liberal Party, but, said Costello, it never came, and the result is a government struggling to manage deep differences over social issues. There was 'jobs and growth', but this is really just a goal without much of a story about how to get there, except for the company tax cuts.

The big question, though, is why the government does not have a coherent economic narrative.

One possible answer is that it has been too preoccupied with social issues such as religious freedom and, before that, same-sex marriage, to give the economy sufficient attention. There is something in that.

But this does not get to the heart of the problem, which is the inability of the Coalition to face the reality of climate change, and its stubborn determination to live in a parallel universe of business as usual. It is climate change denial that is preventing the government from developing a coherent economic narrative.

To be sure, those who doubt the seriousness of climate change are now more likely to describe themselves as sceptics rather than outright deniers, but the effects are the same. Doubting the risks of climate change, opposing serious counter-measures and believing in coal's long-term future is an identity issue for many Coalition politicians.

As an identity issue, it is largely impervious to evidence, as we saw in government ministers' hasty dismissal of the recent Intergovernmental Panel on Climate Change report – before they had even read it, one suspects. Identity issues are also resistant to the normal processes of bargaining and compromise with which many political conflicts are resolved. The National Energy Guarantee was the last of the government's energy policies to founder on the suspicion that a market mechanism might damage coal. Chief Scientist Alan Finkel's Clean Energy Target met the same fate.

So, now, some members of the party of private enterprise and the free market, which argued for and oversaw the privatisation of most of Australia's power utilities, are seriously advocating that the government develop a coal-fired power station. Former Deputy Prime Minister Barnaby Joyce has been at it again in recent weeks.

When AGL announced the planned closure of its ageing Liddell coal-fired power station last year, the government strenuously tried to dissuade it, keep it running for longer or to sell it to rival power company Alinta. The pressure was very public on AGL to 'do the right thing', but also private, with Prime Minister Malcolm Turnbull ringing AGL Chairman Graeme Hunt. It was to no avail, and AGL persisted with its commercially based decision to close the plant and invest instead in the generation of renewable energy, as it had every right to do.

To state the obvious, the stubborn commitment to coal is pulling the government's economic policy towards the sort of state socialism it is supposed to abhor. No wonder it is having difficulty developing a coherent economic narrative.

Further, it is alienating the government, and the Liberal Party in particular, from its natural supporters in the business community. With the collapse of the NEG, the government has no energy policy to provide certainty to business and investors. The focus of the new Minister for Energy, Angus Taylor, has contracted to reducing power prices for consumers. Climate policy has been shifted back into the portfolio of the Minister for the Environment, separating energy from emissions and further demonstrating the identity denialism that distorts the government's economic narrative. Faced with doubts about Australia's capacity to meet its agreed Paris targets, the government blithely says we are 'on track'.

But most big business, outside the fossil fuel industry, is not in denial about the real risks of climate change, nor the imperatives of international action. Since Turnbull walked away from the NEG in a vain attempt to appease his critics and save his leadership, the Australian Industry Group and the Business Council of Australia have both been discussing ways to 'go it alone' on emissions reduction.

Australian Financial Review journalist Phil Coorey last week quoted a member of the Business Council of Australia's Energy and Climate

Change Committee: 'Someone has got to do something. This has to be industry-led unless government wants to take over the markets.'

Industry needs certainty to invest, and to maintain and create the jobs that are central to the government's focus on 'jobs and growth'. That certainty needs to last beyond the tenure of one government or even two, and have bipartisan support.

Yet, the government is unwilling to provide that certainty. As Angus Taylor told an AFR National Energy Summit last week: 'There is no room for bipartisanship when we have a 26% [reduction target] and the other side has 45%.'

But because climate policy has become an identity issue for some members of the Coalition, and they fight about it tooth and nail, it has been removed from the normal processes of policy formation.

No wonder the government can't develop a coherent economic narrative.

The vomit principle, the dead bat, the freeze: How political spin doctors' tactics aim to shape the news

Caroline Fisher
Assistant Professor in Journalism, University of Canberra

1 February 2019

It's election season again and, behind the scenes, the political 'spin doctors' are working around the clock.

They are the campaign advisers, social media strategists, press secretaries and others who craft political messages to help 'sell' their candidate. The term 'spin' is contested, of course, and, like the phrase 'fake news', has become an easy retort for people who reject any version of events that does not reflect their own.

But the fact is any good spin doctor employs a range of overt and covert tactics to get their message across, and I've listed some below.

This list is drawn from a range of academic and other sources (for example, 'Spin: From tactic to tabloid' by Leighton Andrews), and my own personal experience as a 'spin doctor'. (I was once a media adviser to Labor's Anna Bligh, a former Queensland Premier.) It is by no means exhaustive, but it provides an overview of some of the traditional tactics employed by political media advisers and politicians.

Overt and covert spin tactics

British researcher Ivor Gaber talked about 'overt' and 'covert' tactics used by press secretaries in Tony Blair's government in the UK.

Overt refers to standard or benign public relations tactics, such as writing press releases, staging events, giving speeches and appearing in the media.

Covert, on the other hand, refers to a range of cynical techniques to manage information – these are the more malign tactics most people associate with 'spin'.

The list below contains a wide range of 'covert' tactics drawn from a range of research and personal experience. Each of these tactics is employed in a bid to exert control over the way the news media report the message:

- the leak: these are strategic leaks offered by politicians or their staff to journalists, in exchange for no scrutiny. In other words, you only get the leak if you promise not to seek comment from the opposing side, or other critics. This is increasing and is a real problem;
- the freeze: punishing journalists for negative reporting;
- the spray: a form of bullying and intimidation, this is another way of punishing journalists for negative coverage. Many political reporters who file an unfavourable story can expect to 'cop a spray' over the phone after it's published;
- the drip: the act of keeping favoured reporters on a drip of exclusive information;
- staying on message: the goal of every public appearance or interview by a politician. In itself, it's not a malign tactic, but the constant repetition of the same messages without answering questions can be a form of obfuscation;
- pivoting: this refers to politicians shifting away from a difficult question or issue to the one he or she wants to talk about;
- the vomit principle: this rule of thumb is widely referred to in political offices. The idea is that if you repeat something so often

you feel like vomiting, only then is it likely to be cutting through with the public;

- playing a dead bat: this refers to not responding to a media inquiry or giving a minimal response in an effort to kill the story;
- the truth, but not the whole truth: this refers to being selective with what one reveals, sharing only the most beneficial or least damaging information;
- throwing out the bodies/taking out the garbage: these tactics are used to disclose damaging information under the cover of a major distraction. The classic example often used was carried out by Jo Moore, a media adviser in the Blair government. On the day of the 9/11 attacks she sent out an email saying: 'It is now a very good day to get out anything we want to bury. Councillors expenses?' Other common days to bury bad news are Christmas Eve, New Year's Eve, grand final day, Melbourne Cup day, or a distraction like a royal visit;
- get rid of it now: the aim of this tactic is to release all of the damaging information on an issue at one time, so the negative story can be dealt with quickly rather than allowing it to bleed on for weeks in the media. One media adviser I interviewed explained it like this: 'It's a truism in politics – if you've got to eat a shit sandwich you've got to eat it straight away ... The advice was always, "Get rid of it now. Go and deal with it now."';
- fire-breaking: setting up or staging a diversion to distract attention away from another issue. In the film *Wag the Dog*, the US President fabricates a war in Albania to distract from a sex scandal. Less extreme examples would be launching a new policy to distract from a negative issue in an attempt to shift the media's attention;
- kite-flying: this means testing or floating an idea before making a commitment to announce it;
- feeding or starving a story: feeding a story means keeping it alive by commenting on it in the media. Starving a story means starving it of oxygen by not commenting on it. The theory being that, after a while, the media will get bored and move on;
- keeping out of the media/being a small target: this is a useful tactic if the politician is unpopular and affects the polls, has a controversial portfolio or is an accident-prone, poor performer;

- flying under the radar: this refers to just quietly getting on with things without publicising it;
- dishing dirt: this is where old claims suddenly emerge publicly before or during an election in an effort to smear someone's reputation. The 'dirt' can come from outside or inside a party. It's a tactic used to try to destroy someone's career;
- dog-whistling: using specific subtle language and messages to target a particular section of the audience (see 'Why politicians love to play the wedge-and-block game' by Ross Gittins);
- wedging: this tactic involves raising an issue that is popular in the electorate and sensitive to the party you are opposing, to 'wedge' them in to a difficult position and sow division in the party.

The list goes on, and will continue to evolve, as spin doctors exploit new media platforms to get the message out. So, next time you hear a politician make a claim, remember to scrutinise what they have said, and consider why, how and when they are saying it. There is nothing wrong with a politician 'putting their best foot forward' and selling their policies. It is essential! After all, the contest of ideas is central to democracy and getting elected. Spin tactics are designed to get your attention, but some are less benevolent than others. So, dig deeper than the limited media coverage, the social media posts, the election ads and the stunts. Check the websites of politicians and their parties for solid policy ideas. Go and talk to candidates outside the shopping centre and test their commitment beyond the spin.

PART VII

Our natural world

The gloves are off: 'Predatory' climate deniers are a threat to our children

Tim Flannery
Professorial Fellow, Melbourne Sustainable Society Institute, University of Melbourne

17 September 2019

In this age of rapidly melting glaciers, terrifying megafires and ever more puissant hurricanes, of acidifying and rising oceans, it is hard to believe any further prod to climate action is needed.

But the reality is, we continue to live in a business-as-usual world. Our media is filled with enthusiastic announcements about new fossil fuel projects, or the unveiling of the latest fossil-fuelled supercar, as if there's no relationship between such things and climate change.

In Australia, the disconnect among our political leaders on the deadly nature of fossil fuels is particularly breathtaking.

Prime Minister Scott Morrison continues to sing the praises of coal, while members of the government call for subsidies for coal-fired power plants. A few days ago, Energy and Emissions Reduction Minister Angus Taylor urged that the nation's old and polluting coal-fired power plants be allowed to run 'at full tilt'.

In the past, many of us have tolerated such pronouncements as the utterings of idiots – in the true, original Greek meaning of the word, of one interested only in their own business. But the climate crisis has now grown so severe that the actions of the denialists have turned predatory: they are now an immediate threat to our children.

A 'colossal failure' of climate activism

Each year the situation becomes more critical. In 2018, global emissions of greenhouse gases rose by 1.7 per cent while the concentration of carbon dioxide in the atmosphere jumped by 3.5 parts per million – the largest-ever observed increase.

No climate report or warning, no political agreement nor technological innovation, has altered the ever-upward trajectory of the pollution. This simple fact forces me to look back on my twenty years of climate activism as a colossal failure.

Many climate scientists think we are already so far down the path of destruction it is impossible to stabilise the global temperature at 1.5 degrees above the pre-industrial average without yet-to-be developed drawdown technologies, such as those that remove greenhouse gases from the atmosphere. On current trends, within a decade or so, stabilising at 2 degrees will likewise be beyond our grasp.

And on the other side of that threshold, nature's positive feedback loops promise to fling us into a hostile world. By 2100 – just eighty years away – if our trajectory does not change, it is estimated Earth will be 4 degrees warmer than it was before we began burning fossil fuels.

Far fewer humans will survive on our warming planet

That future Earth may have enough resources to support far fewer people than the 7.6 billion it supports today. British scientist James Lovelock has predicted a future human population of just a billion people. Mass deaths are predicted to result from, among other causes, disease outbreaks, air pollution, malnutrition and starvation, heatwaves and suicide.

My children, and those of many prominent polluters and climate denialists, will probably live to be part of that grim winnowing – a world that the Alan Joneses and Andrew Bolts of the world have laboured so hard to create.

How should Australia's parents deal with those who labour so joyously to create a world in which a large portion of humanity will perish? As I have become ever more furious at the polluters and denialists, I have come to understand they are threatening my children's wellbeing as much as anyone who might seek to harm a child.

Young people themselves are now mobilising against the danger. Increasingly they're giving up on words and resorting to actions. Extinction Rebellion is the Anthropocene's answer to the UK working class Chartists, the US Declaration of Independence and the defenders of the Eureka Stockade.

Its declaration states:

> This is our darkest hour. Humanity finds itself embroiled in an event unprecedented in its history, one which, unless immediately addressed, will catapult us further into the destruction of all we hold dear [...] The wilful complicity displayed by our government has shattered

> meaningful democracy and cast aside the common interest in favour of short-term gain and private profit [...] We hereby declare the bonds of the social contract to be null and void.

Words have not cut through. Is rebellion the only option?

Not yet a year old, Extinction Rebellion has had an enormous impact. In April it shut down six critical locations in London, such as Piccadilly Circus, overwhelmed the police and justice system with 1000 arrests, and forced the British government to become the first nation ever to declare a climate emergency.

So unstable is our current societal response that a single young woman, Greta Thunberg, has been able to spark a profoundly powerful global movement. Less than a year ago, she went on a one-person school strike. Today, school strikes for climate action are a global phenomenon.

On 20 September in Australia and elsewhere, school principals must decide whether they will allow their students to march in the global climate strike in an effort to save themselves from the climate predators in our midst, or force them to stay and study for a future that will not, on current trends, eventuate.

I will be marching with the strikers in Melbourne, and I believe teachers should join their pupils on that day. After all, us older generations should be painfully aware that our efforts have not been enough to protect our children.

The new and carefully planned rebellion by the young generation forces us earlier generations of climate activists to re-examine our strategy. Should we continue to use words to try to win the debate? Or should we become climate rebels? Changing the language around climate denialism will, I hope, sharpen our focus as we ponder what comes next.

One cat, one year, 110 native animals: Lock up your pet, it's a killing machine

Jaana Dielenberg
University Fellow, Charles Darwin University

Brett Murphy
Associate Professor / ARC Future Fellow, Charles Darwin University

Chris Dickman
Professor in Terrestrial Ecology, University of Sydney

John Woinarski
Professor (conservation biology), Charles Darwin University

Leigh-Ann Woolley
Adjunct Research Associate, Charles Darwin University

Mike Calver
Associate Professor in Biological Sciences, Murdoch University

Sarah Legge
Professor, Australian National University

14 May 2020

We know feral cats are an enormous problem for wildlife – across Australia, feral cats collectively kill more than three billion animals per year.

Cats have played a leading role in most of Australia's thirty-four mammal extinctions since 1788, and are a big reason populations of at least 123 other threatened native species are dropping.

But pet cats are wreaking havoc too. Our new analysis compiles the results of sixty-six different studies on pet cats to gauge the impact of Australia's pet cat population on the country's wildlife.

The results are staggering. On average, each roaming pet cat kills 186 reptiles, birds and mammals per year, most of them native to Australia. Collectively, that's 4440 to 8100 animals per square kilometre per year for the area inhabited by pet cats.

If you own a cat and want to protect wildlife, you should keep it inside. In Australia, 1.1 million pet cats are contained twenty-four hours a day by responsible pet owners. The remaining 2.7 million pet cats – 71 per cent of all pet cats – are able to roam and hunt.

What's more, your pet cat could be getting out without you knowing. A radio tracking study in Adelaide found that of the 177 cats whom owners believed were inside at night, sixty-nine cats (39 per cent) were sneaking out for nocturnal adventures. (See 'Cat Tracker South Australia: Understanding pet cats through citizen science' by Philip Roetman et al.)

Surely not my cat

Just over one-quarter of Australian households (27 per cent) have pet cats, and about half of cat-owning households have two or more cats.

Many owners believe their animals don't hunt because they never come across evidence of killed animals.

But studies that used cat video tracking collars or scat analysis (checking what's in the cat's poo) have established many pet cats kill animals without bringing them home. On average, pet cats bring home only 15 per cent of their prey.

Collectively, roaming pet cats kill 390 million animals per year in Australia.

This huge number may lead some pet owners to think the contribution of their own cat wouldn't make much difference. However, we found even single pet cats have driven declines and complete losses of populations of some native animal species in their area.

Documented cases have included: a feather-tailed glider population in south-eastern NSW; a skink population in a Perth suburb; and an olive legless lizard population in Canberra.

Urban cats

On average, an individual feral cat in the bush kills 748 reptiles, birds and mammals a year – four times the toll of a hunting pet cat. But feral cats and pet cats roam over very different areas.

Pet cats are confined to cities and towns, where you'll find forty to seventy roaming cats per square kilometre. In the bush there's only one feral cat for every 3 to 4 square kilometres.

So, while each pet cat kills fewer animals than a feral cat, their high urban density means the toll is still very high. Per square kilometre per year, pet cats kill thirty–fifty times more animals than feral cats in the bush.

Most of us want to see native wildlife around towns and cities. But such a vision is being compromised by this extraordinary level of predation, especially as the human population grows and our cities expand.

Many native animals don't have high reproductive rates, so they cannot survive this level of predation. The stakes are especially high for threatened wildlife in urban areas.

Pet cats living near areas with nature also hunt more, reducing the value of places that should be safe havens for wildlife.

The 186 animals each pet cat kills per year on average is made up of 110 native animals (forty reptiles, thirty-eight birds and thirty-two mammals).

For example, the critically endangered western ringtail possum is found in suburban areas of Mandurah, Bunbury, Busselton and Albany in Western Australia. The possum did not move into these areas – rather, we moved into their habitat.

What can pet owners do?

Keeping your cat securely contained twenty-four hours a day is the only way to prevent it from killing wildlife.

It's a myth that a good diet or feeding a cat more meat will prevent hunting: even cats that aren't hungry will hunt.

Various devices, such as bells on collars, are commercially marketed with the promise of preventing hunting. While some of these items may reduce the rate of successful kills, they don't prevent hunting altogether.

And they don't prevent cats from disturbing wildlife. When cats prowl and hunt in an area, wildlife have to spend more time hiding or escaping. This reduces the time spent feeding themselves or their young, or resting.

In Mandurah, the disturbance and hunting of just one pet cat and one stray cat caused the total breeding failure of a colony of more than 100 pairs of fairy terns.

Benefits of a life indoors

Keeping pet cats indoors protects them from injury, avoids nuisance behaviour and prevents unwanted breeding.

Cats allowed outside often get into fights with other cats, even when they're not the fighting type (they can be attacked by other cats when running away).

Roaming cats are also very prone to getting hit by a vehicle. According to the Humane Society of the United States, indoor cats live up to four times longer than those allowed to roam freely.

Indoor cats have lower rates of cat-borne diseases, some of which can infect humans. For example, in humans the cat-borne disease toxoplasmosis can cause illness, miscarriages and birth defects.

But Australia is in a very good position to make change. Compared with many other countries, the Australian public are more aware of how cats threaten native wildlife and more supportive of actions to reduce those impacts.

It won't be easy. But since more than one million pet cats are already being contained, reducing the impacts from pet cats is clearly possible if we take responsibility for them.

Australia, you have unfinished business. It's time to let our 'fire people' care for this land

David Bowman
Professor of Pyrogeography and Fire Science, University of Tasmania
Greg Lehman
Pro Vice Chancellor, Aboriginal Leadership, University of Tasmania
Andry Sculthorpe
The Tasmanian Aboriginal Centre

28 May 2020

Since last summer's bushfire crisis, there's been a quantum shift in public awareness of Aboriginal fire management. It's now more widely understood that Aboriginal people used landscape burning to sustain biodiversity and suppress large bushfires.

The Morrison government's bushfire royal commission, which began hearings this week, recognises the potential of incorporating Aboriginal knowledge into mainstream fire management.

Its terms of reference seek to understand ways 'the traditional land and fire management practices of Indigenous Australians could improve Australia's resilience to natural disasters'.

Incorporating Aboriginal knowledge is essential to tackling future bushfire crises. But it risks perpetuating historical injustices, by appropriating Aboriginal knowledge without recognition or compensation. So, while the bushfire threat demands urgent action, we must also take care.

Accommodating traditional fire knowledge is a long-overdue accompaniment to recent advances in land rights and native title. It is an essential part of the unfinished business of post-colonial Australia.

A living record

Before 1788, Aboriginal cultures across Australia used fire to deliberately and skilfully manage the bush.

Broadly, it involved numerous, frequent fires that created fine-scale mosaics of burnt and unburnt patches. Developed over thousands of years, such burning made intense bushfires uncommon, and made plant and animal foods more abundant. This benefited wildlife and sustained a biodiversity of animals and plants.

Following European settlement, Aboriginal people were dispossessed of their land and the opportunity to manage it with fire. Since then, the Australian bush has seen dramatic biodiversity declines, tree invasion of grasslands, and more frequent and destructive bushfires.

In many parts of Australia, particularly densely settled areas, cultural burning practices have been severely disrupted. But in some regions, such as clan estates in Arnhem Land, unbroken traditions of fire management date back to the mid to late Pleistocene, some 50,000 years ago.

Not all nations can draw on these living records of traditional fire management.

Indigenous people around the world, including in western Europe, used fire to manage flammable landscapes. But industrialisation, intensive agriculture and colonisation led to these practices being lost.

In most cases, historical records are the only way to learn about them.

Rising from the ashes

In Australia, many Aboriginal people are rekindling cultural practices, sometimes in collaboration with non-Indigenous land managers. They are drawing on retained community knowledge of past fire practices – and in some cases, embracing practices from other regions.

Burning programs can be adapted to the challenges of a rapidly changing world. These include the need to protect assets; and new threats such as weeds, climate change, forest disturbances from logging and fire, and feral animals.

This process is outlined well in Victor Steffensen's recent book *Fire Country: How Indigenous Fire Management Could Help Save Australia.* Steffensen describes how, as an Aboriginal man born into two cultures, he made a journey of self-discovery – learning about fire management while being guided and mentored by two Aboriginal elders.

Together, they reintroduced fire into traditional lands on Cape York. These practices had been prohibited after European-based systems of land tenure and management were imposed.

Steffensen extended his experience to cultural renewal and ecological restoration across Australia, arguing this was critical to addressing the bushfire crisis:

> The bottom line for me is that we need to work towards a whole other division of fire managers on the land ... A skilled team of Indigenous and non-Indigenous people that works with the entire community, agencies and emergency services to deliver an effective and educational strategy into the future. One that is culturally based and connects to all the benefits for the community.

Making it happen

How do we realise this ideal? Explicit affirmative action policies, funded by state and federal governments, are a practical way to protect and extend Aboriginal burning cultures.

Specifically, such programs should provide ways for Aboriginal people and communities to:

- develop their fire management knowledge and capacity
- maintain and renew traditional cultural practices
- enter mainstream fire management, including in leadership roles
- enter a broad cross-section of agencies, and community groups involved in fire management.

This will require rapidly building capacity to train and employ Aboriginal fire practitioners.

In some instances, where the impact of colonisation has been most intense, action is needed to support Aboriginal communities to re-establish relationships with forested areas, following generations of forced removal from their Country.

Importantly, this empowerment will enable Aboriginal communities to re-establish their own cultural priorities and practices in caring for Country. Where these differ from the Eurocentric values of mainstream Australia, we must understand and respect the wisdom of those who have been custodians of this flammable landscape for millennia.

Non-Indigenous Australians should also pay for these ancient skills. Funding schemes could include training, and ensuring affirmative action programs are implemented and achieve their goals.

Involving Aboriginal people and communities in the development of fire management will ensure cultural knowledge is shared on culturally agreed terms.

Fire people, fire country

In many ways, last summer's fire season is a reminder of the brutal acquisition of land in Australia and its ongoing consequences for all Australians.

The challenges involved in helping to right this wrong, by enabling Aboriginal people to use their fire management practices, are complex. They span social justice, funding, legal liability, cultural rights, fire management and science.

Fundamentally, we must recognise Aborigines are 'fire people' who live on 'fire country'. It's time to embrace this ancient fact.

How to kill fruit flies, according to a scientist

Thomas Merritt
Professor and Canada Research Chair, Chemistry and Biochemistry, Laurentian University

9 August 2017

As a researcher who works on fruit flies, I am often asked how to get them out of someone's kitchen. This happens to fly researchers often enough that we sit around fly conferences (these actually exist) and complain about getting asked this question.

Meanwhile, we watch the same fruit flies buzz around our beers, instead of discussing pithy and insightful questions about the research that we're pursuing.

But I get it: fruit flies are annoying. So, fine, here's how we get rid of them in my lab: we build a trap. It's not perfect, but it's okay.

1. Take a small jar (we use small canning jars) and pour in cider vinegar to about 2 centimetres deep.
2. 'Cap' the jar with a funnel. You can use a plastic funnel if you have one, but a makeshift paper one works well.
3. Tape the funnel in place, so there are no gaps for the flies to crawl out.
4. Flies fly in and can't find their way out. Every day or two, replace the vinegar.

Instead of vinegar, you can also use beer or wine, but I prefer to drink one of these while making the traps.

There is actually a little science behind the trap. Fruit flies – at least, *Drosophila melanogaster*, the most common fly buzzing around your bananas – are attracted to ageing fruit; rotting fruit, in particular. They lay their eggs there, and the larvae hatch and feed on the soft, overripe flesh.

To find that fruit, flies use their sense of smell: what we call their olfactory system. What they are sensing, smelling, are things like acetic acid – the molecule that gives vinegar its pungent punch. You could bait your trap with fruit, but vinegar jumps right to the chase and lures them in.

The flies flying around your kitchen likely came from outside. *Drosophila melanogaster* are originally an African species, but they've spread across the globe. We call them a 'cosmopolitan' species – they're found wherever people are.

Where flies come from and why we research them

The story of how they've adapted to so many different environments (like, for example, the tip of Florida or even northern Ontario, where I live) is an interesting one and a hot topic of current research. The flies that buzz around my fruit bowl, at least in the summer and fall, likely came from a local population. I've actually done work on flies we collected from the composter in my backyard.

Interestingly, the combination of a tropical species, a cool day and a warm house is likely why there seem to be more flies in the fall. As the temperature outside goes down (and even on cool summer nights where I live), the flies come inside where it's warm. Where do the flies go in the winter? We actually don't know. We know they can't freeze and live, so our best guess is they hide away in basements, waiting for warm weather. There's actually a name for this idea. We call it the 'Root Cellar Hypothesis'.

The second question that I, and every other fly researcher, get asked is: why flies? Good question. The first answer is: because they're small. Seriously.

Much of the research I do involves asking how individuals, or small groups of individuals, are similar and different. Asking this question is best done with thousands of individuals. An average experiment in my lab can involve tens of thousands of flies. Imagine doing this kind of work on zebras. That's a lot of zebras. It also helps that flies grow quickly, reproduce constantly and are super easy (usually) to keep in the lab.

The second reason why we research flies is because they are strikingly similar to humans – or any other animal on our planet. Because life on Earth shares a common ancestry, we have all evolved in complex and interwoven paths from a common ancestor. We share much of our genetics and almost all of our biochemistry.

Some 60–80 per cent of genes found in humans are found in flies, and essentially all our biochemistry and metabolism is identical. When we ask a question using flies, we can answer a question that interests us about humans.

It is this relatedness, and the ease of working with them in the lab, that has led to research on flies being the foundation of no fewer than four Nobel prizes.

Ironically, as I type this, there is literally a fruit fly – *Drosophila melanogaster* – walking the lip of my coffee cup. The little devils are everywhere.

Worried about Earth's future? Well, the outlook is worse than even scientists can grasp

Corey JA Bradshaw
Matthew Flinders Professor of Global Ecology and Models Theme Leader for the ARC Centre of Excellence for Australian Biodiversity and Heritage, Flinders University

Daniel T Blumstein
Professor in the Department of Ecology and Evolutionary Biology and the Institute of the Environment and Sustainability, University of California, Los Angeles

Paul Ehrlich
President, Center for Conservation Biology, Bing Professor of Population Studies, Stanford University

13 January 2021

Anyone with even a passing interest in the global environment knows all is not well. But just how bad is the situation? Our new paper, 'Underestimating the challenges of avoiding a ghastly future', shows the outlook for life on Earth is more dire than is generally understood.

Our research, published today, reviews more than 150 studies to produce a stark summary of the state of the natural world. We outline the likely future trends in biodiversity decline, mass extinction, climate disruption and planetary toxification. We clarify the gravity of the human predicament and provide a timely snapshot of the crises that must be addressed now.

The problems, all tied to human consumption and population growth, will almost certainly worsen over coming decades. The damage will be felt for centuries and threatens the survival of all species, including our own.

Our paper was authored by seventeen leading scientists, including those from Flinders University, Stanford University and the University of California, Los Angeles. Our message might not be popular, and, indeed, is frightening. But scientists must be candid and accurate if humanity is to understand the enormity of the challenges we face.

Getting to grips with the problem

First, we reviewed the extent to which experts grasp the scale of the threats to the biosphere and its life forms, including humanity. Alarmingly, the research shows future environmental conditions will be far more dangerous than experts currently believe.

This is largely because academics tend to specialise in one discipline, which means they are, in many cases, unfamiliar with the complex system in which planetary-scale problems – and their potential solutions – exist.

What's more, positive change can be impeded by governments rejecting or ignoring scientific advice, and ignorance of human behaviour by both technical experts and policy makers.

More broadly, the human optimism bias – thinking bad things are more likely to befall others than yourself – means many people underestimate the environmental crisis.

Numbers don't lie

Our research also reviewed the current state of the global environment. While the problems are too numerous to cover in full here, they include:

- a halving of vegetation biomass since the agricultural revolution around 11,000 years ago. Overall, humans have altered almost two-thirds of Earth's land surface;
- about 1300 documented species extinctions over the past 500 years, with many more unrecorded. More broadly, population sizes of animal species have declined by more than two-thirds over the past fifty years, suggesting more extinctions are imminent;
- about one million plant and animal species globally threatened with extinction. The combined mass of wild mammals today is less than one-quarter the mass before humans started colonising the planet. Insects are also disappearing rapidly in many regions;
- 85 per cent of the global wetland area lost in 300 years, and more than 65 per cent of the oceans compromised to some extent by humans;
- a halving of live coral cover on reefs in less than 200 years and a decrease in seagrass extent by 10 per cent per decade over the last century. About 40 per cent of kelp forests have declined in abundance, and the number of large predatory fishes is less than 30 per cent of that a century ago.

A bad situation only getting worse

The human population has reached 7.8 billion – double what it was in 1970 – and is set to reach about 10 billion by 2050. More people equals more food insecurity, soil degradation, plastic pollution and biodiversity loss.

High population densities make pandemics more likely. They also drive overcrowding, unemployment, housing shortages and deteriorating infrastructure, and can spark conflicts leading to insurrections, terrorism and war.

Essentially, humans have created an ecological Ponzi scheme. Consumption, as a percentage of Earth's capacity to regenerate itself, has grown from 73 per cent in 1960 to more than 170 per cent today.

High-consuming countries like Australia, Canada and the US use multiple units of fossil-fuel energy to produce one energy unit of food. Energy consumption will therefore increase in the near future, especially as the global middle class grows.

Then there's climate change. Humanity has already exceeded global warming of 1 degree Celsius this century and will almost assuredly exceed 1.5 degrees Celsius between 2030 and 2052. Even if all nations party to the Paris Agreement ratify their commitments, warming would still reach between 2.6 and 3.1 degrees Celsius by 2100.

The danger of political impotence

Our paper found global policy-making falls far short of addressing these existential threats. Securing Earth's future requires prudent, long-term decisions. However, this is impeded by short-term interests, and an economic system that concentrates wealth among a few individuals.

Right-wing populist leaders with anti-environment agendas are on the rise, and in many countries, environmental protest groups have been labelled 'terrorists'. Environmentalism has become weaponised as a political ideology, rather than properly viewed as a universal mode of self-preservation.

Financed disinformation campaigns, such as those against climate action and forest protection, protect short-term profits and claim meaningful environmental action is too costly – while ignoring the broader cost of not acting. By and large, it appears unlikely business investments will shift at sufficient scale to avoid environmental catastrophe.

Changing course

Fundamental change is required to avoid this ghastly future. Specifically, we and many others suggest:

- abolishing the goal of perpetual economic growth

- revealing the true cost of products and activities by forcing those who damage the environment to pay for its restoration, such as through carbon pricing
- rapidly eliminating fossil fuels
- regulating markets by curtailing monopolisation and limiting undue corporate influence on policy
- reining in corporate lobbying of political representatives
- educating and empowering women across the globe, including giving them control over family planning.

Don't look away

Many organisations and individuals are devoted to achieving these aims. However, their messages have not sufficiently penetrated the policy, economic, political and academic realms to make much difference.

Failing to acknowledge the magnitude of problems facing humanity is not just naive, it's dangerous. And science has a big role to play here.

Scientists must not sugar-coat the overwhelming challenges ahead. Instead, they should *tell it like it is*. Anything else is at best misleading, and at worst potentially lethal for the human enterprise.

I've always wondered: Who would win in a fight between the black mamba and the inland taipan?

Timothy NW Jackson
Postdoctoral Research Fellow, Australian Venom Research Unit, University of Melbourne

21 February 2020

I've Always Wondered is a series by The Conversation where readers send in questions they'd like an expert to answer.

Who would win in a fight between the black mamba and the inland taipan? – Biswajit Tripathy

Dear Biswajit,

What a fascinating question!

Before we start talking about the fight, we first need to think about why these two snakes got into the dust-up. Despite what many people think, snakes are generally very shy and cautious animals that will do their very best to avoid trouble.

This is sensible – why take the risk of getting hurt if you can avoid it?

Having said that, there are two main reasons why snakes get into fights with other snakes. During the breeding season, male snakes sometimes fight other male snakes of the same species.

We might think of this as a way of impressing the girls – not a good reason for a fight between two humans, but it seems to work for snakes. Because black mambas and inland taipans are two different species, though, we can rule out this reason for their biff.

The most likely reason for our showdown is that one snake is trying to eat the other.

A serving of snake might not seem very appetising to us, but a smaller snake is actually a very nice meal for a larger snake. Some species of snakes, like the king cobra, even specialise in eating other snakes – they are extremely fussy about their food and turn their noses up at almost any other meal.

Black mambas normally eat mammals and birds, and inland taipans almost exclusively eat mammals like rats and mice, but most snakes will take advantage of an easy meal if it presents itself.

Before we get to the fun bit, we should note that black mambas are from Africa and inland taipans are from Australia. This means, under natural circumstances, the two species would never meet.

In fact, black mambas and inland taipans are like the 'alpha' snakes of Africa and Australia. They're the top dogs of their turf and, once they become adult snakes, there aren't too many other animals that want to tangle with them.

The battle

The stage is set, the combatants have entered the ring, there can be only one winner. Which will it be?

Snakes have two main ways of fighting: they can wrestle and they can bite. When boy snakes fight to impress the girls, they usually just wrestle, wrapping around and around each other to see who's strongest, as each tries to pin his opponent's head to the ground.

When snakes fight because one thinks the other would make a yummy snake snack, they fight dirty, by any means necessary, both wrestling and

(Wes Mountain/
The Conversation)

biting. Black mambas and inland taipans are both famously venomous, so their bites pack a serious punch!

But which venom is the more powerful weapon? Which one will give its owner the edge?

Taipan venom is extremely strong – it's the most powerful snake venom there is, at least against mice. Black mamba venom, on the other hand, is extremely fast-acting.

We have good reason to believe taipan venom is specially designed for taking down rats as quickly as possible. But the way they do that – by interfering with the rat's blood – probably won't work well against the mamba.

Black mamba venom is designed for rapidly taking down birds as well as mammals, and this turns out to be an important point. If you've seen *Jurassic Park* (if you haven't, stop whatever you're doing and see it immediately!), you know birds are descended from dinosaurs.

In fact, even though birds have feathers and (usually) fly, they're actually just a special group of reptiles. Birds are more closely related to crocodiles than crocodiles are to lizards! This means that a venom that works well against birds probably works well against most other reptiles, including snakes.

The mamba has the edge when it comes to venom – watch out, inland taipan!

Wrestling is important too. And although mambas can grow very long and are very fast, taipans have more muscle and are probably stronger.

(Wes Mountain/
The Conversation)

If the taipan was very careful not to get bitten during the scuffle, there's a good chance it could overpower the mamba – watch out, black mamba!

Sizing up the opponent

These species are closely matched, each with their own special weapon they could use to win the fight. Remember, the reason these snakes are fighting is because one wants to eat the other, and only a silly snake – one with eyes bigger than its stomach – would try to eat a snake bigger than itself.

So, who would win?

Although both species are highly venomous and each of their venoms is beautifully designed for subduing their natural prey, the biological reality is that the winner would probably be whichever snake was bigger on the day, regardless of species.

This is an important lesson for us about snakes – despite their impressively toxic venoms, they generally do not like to pick fights with animals that are much bigger than they are.

Since we humans are a *lot* bigger than snakes, they'd much prefer to hide from us and get out of our way as fast as possible. If we leave snakes alone, they will leave us alone – look, but don't touch!

Even though our fantasy fight between the black mamba and inland taipan might never happen in reality, this was a great question because it made us think about snake biology, from behaviour to venom, in a fun way. Using our imagination to learn about the natural world is never a bad thing.

Seaweed, Indonesia's answer to the global plastic crisis

Bakti Berlyanto Sedayu
PhD Candidate, Victoria University

4 June 2018

The impacts of global plastic use have reached an alarming level. Based on the latest data, 9 billion tonnes of plastics have been produced since the 1950s, creating 7 billion tonnes of waste. Plastic waste not only damages the environment and threatens animal life but also harms human populations.

One of the most dangerous elements of plastic waste is tiny pieces of debris known as microplastics. These are damaging the environment, mostly the ocean, and in much greater amounts than originally thought. A recent study shows the number of microplastics has reached up to 51 trillion particles, or 236,000 metric tonnes, globally. (See 'A global inventory of small floating plastic debris' by Erik van Sebille et al.) These tiny particles can end up in people's stomachs via drinking water or eating seafood, which could present health risks. (See 'Potential health impact of environmentally released micro- and nanoplastics in the human food production chain: Experiences from nanotoxicology' by Hans Bouwmeester et al.)

Various attempts to minimise plastic use have been introduced. One involves developing plastic materials, known as biodegradable plastics or bioplastics, that decompose naturally in the environment.

My research aims to show how seaweed can be the best material for use in bioplastics. Indonesia could play a key role in developing seaweed-based plastics.

Policies against plastic

A number of countries have recently introduced policies to encourage the use of degradable plastics and recycling to minimise plastic use.

The UK will ban all sales of single-use plastic, including plastic straws and cotton swabs, next year.

Cities in the US have declared war on plastic straws. Seattle has launched a campaign dubbed 'Strawless in Seattle', while New York is considering a ban on plastic straws.

In 2017, Kenya introduced the toughest plastic bag ban, with a penalty of four years in jail or a $40,000 fine.

Finding solutions

However, it is impossible to stop plastic use.

So far, plastic is the most convenient and versatile material for various purposes and brings huge benefits to our lives. People's continued dependency on plastic has encouraged the rise in its production.

The plastic industry is huge and is expected to continue expanding. In 2014, the plastic packaging industry was valued at US$270 billion and this is projected to increase to $375 billion by 2030.

One way to control plastic use is through recycling. However, things are not as easy as expected. Plastic products come in a hundred or more varieties. These variations are so huge it is difficult to sort them out for the recycling process.

Therefore, only about 9 per cent of plastic waste is recycled. Around 12 per cent is incinerated. The rest ends up mostly in landfill or the ocean.

Bioplastics offer an alternative. They are commonly made from plants or bacteria and are more environmentally friendly, as well as sustainable.

Strong demand for bioplastics

Global bioplastic production capacity will increase to 6.1 million tonnes in 2021 from 4.2 million tonnes in 2016, due to people's increasing awareness of eco-friendly products.

People have started using bioplastics in their daily lives, with uses ranging from shopping bags and disposable housewares to electronics.

Big brands such as Coca-Cola, Heinz, Unilever, Nestle, Danone and Nike have started using bioplastics for their packaging.

Why seaweed?

The materials commonly used to produce bioplastics are corn, sugarcane, vegetable oil and starch. However, using these ingredients for plastics has raised some concerns.

First, the production of bioplastic requires a huge investment in the land, fertilisers and chemicals. Second, the use of these plants for plastics will trigger a competition between plants for food versus plants for plastics, which could lead to food price hikes and food crises.

Seaweed is, so far, the best candidate for bioplastics, as it manages to answer both of the challenges above. First, it is cheap. Unlike other terrestrial plants, seaweed can grow without fertiliser. It does not take up huge space on land, as it grows offshore. By using seaweed for bioplastics, the production of agricultural commodities for food will remain intact, so no food price hikes or food crisis.

Indonesia's role

Indonesia is the largest archipelago in the world and two-thirds of its territory is water. It is one of the world's largest seaweed producers, accounting for more than a third of global seaweed production. Indonesia's seaweed exports were valued at around US$200 million in 2014, with production reportedly increasing at about 30 per cent per year.

It is also the world's largest producer of red seaweed, whose carbohydrate element is the key ingredient for bioplastics.

A recent report ('UNDP/FAO Regional Seafarming Development and Demonstration Project: A UN report on the development of seaweed farming globally') suggests Indonesia is a highly suitable place for red seaweed farming, due to its climate, nutrients and geographical conditions.

It is also one step ahead of other countries in developing seaweed-based plastics. Indonesian start-up Indonesia Evoware has invented cups and food containers made from farmed seaweeds and sold them commercially.

The invention shows seaweed's huge potential as an alternative material for bioplastics. More research is needed to ensure seaweed-based plastics can be applied to other plastic products. In the future, we hope seaweed-based plastics will be comparable with conventional plastics.

Given its potential, Indonesia should play a key role in developing eco-friendly plastics from seaweed to avert a global plastic crisis. When water bottles or shopping bags from seaweed-based plastics become waste, we will have nothing to worry about, as the waste will just go back to where it came from.